MEMORIZE SIGN LANGUAGE

by Judy Tieso,   Rex S. Story

DILL ENTERPRISES
P.O. BOX 29192
LINCOLN, NEBRASKA 68529

Production- Steve Burnett
Artwork- Carlton Bruett
Linda Tanderup
Scott Pedersen
Becky Roux

84 5774

Special thanks to Jerry K.

ISBN 0-9606504-0-7
SECOND EDITION—FIRST PRINTING
PRINTED IN USA
LIBRARY OF CONGRESS CATALOG NO. **81-82905**

THE AUTHOR   JUDY TIESO

Judy S. Tieso is a Speech/Language Pathologist currently employed by the Lincoln Public Schools, Lincoln, Nebraska. She received her Bachelor of Arts degree from Hastings College and her Master of Arts in Speech Pathology from the University of Nebraska in Lincoln. She served as coordinator of Speech/Language and Audiological Services at the Beatrice State Developmental Center where she developed a system for teaching manual communication skills to deaf, hard of hearing, and non-verbal individuals.

During the past several years, Mrs. Tieso has taught numerous courses in sign language for various agencies including Southeast Community College and the Lincoln Public Schools. She has also served as an interpreter for the deaf at various functions including group meetings and worship services.

THE MEMORY PROCESS   REX S. STORY

Rex Story has been active throughout the United States as a consultant for educational services. He has authored two nationally distributed books and served as publisher and editor of the AAV-WD Magazine. In the past he has conducted management training seminars, cultural exchange workshops, sports seminars and media productions. Rex is currently a college instructor and functions as a consultant in the promotion and development of memory aids.

TABLE OF CONTENTS

THE SIGN ALPHABET...1

ALPHABET REVIEW...10

INTRODUCTION..11

INSTRUCTION GUIDELINES...........................12

LESSON 1 (words)...13

LESSON 1-Review 22

LESSON 2...23

LESSON 2-Review...32

LESSON 3...33

LESSON 3-Review...42

LESSON 4...43

LESSON 4-Review...52

LESSON 5...53

LESSON 5-Review...62

LESSON 6...63

LESSON 6-Review...72

LESSON 7...73

LESSON 7-Review...82

LESSON 8...83

LESSON 8-Review...92

LESSON 9...93

LESSON 9-Review...102

LESSON 10...103

LESSON 10-Review...112

Bibliography..113

Index and Final Review..................................... 114

HOW TO USE THE SIGNTURE© ALPHABET

Rehearse the memory aids in this manner:

step **1.** Say the letter.

step **2.** Sign the letter.

step **3.** Look at the 'signture.' (sign-picture-association)

step **4.** Picture in your mind the signture on your own hand as you sign the letter.

step **5.** Repeat outloud 3 times.

step **6.** Do the entire alphabet in this way.

step **7.** Close the book and review the alphabet.

BASIC RULES—FINGERSPELLING

1. Hold arm comfortably at the waist.
2. Keep palm of your hand facing the person to whom you are spelling.
3. Move fingers smoothly —do not jerk at the wrist or bounce at elbow.
4. Bounce hand slightly or open and close letter to indicate double letters in a word — ball.
5. If having trouble with a letter during practice—hold previous letter in word—don't start over.
6. Practice reading other people and yourself in the mirror.
7. Be exact—speed is not important.
8. When spelling phrases or two words together -give a very slight pause between words.
9. Practice—practice—practice—practice—practice—practice! ! ! ! ! ! !

THE MANUAL SIGN ALPHABET IN PICTURES

A

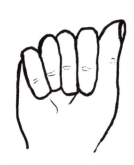

BALANCE ON
THE THUMB AN
APPLE

B

WAVING BYE

C

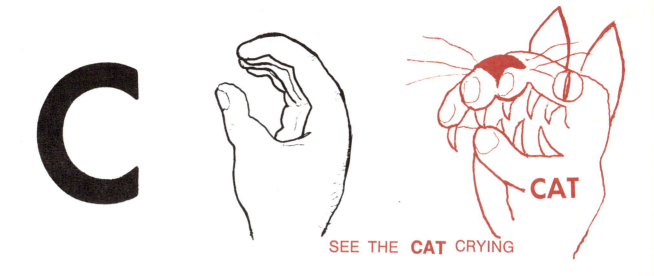

SEE THE **CAT** CRYING

d

PICTURE A **DOG** WITH YOUR
INDEX FINGER AS ITS TAIL.

E

EAT

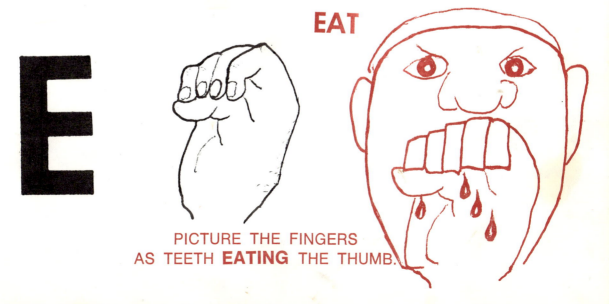

PICTURE THE FINGERS
AS TEETH **EATING** THE THUMB.

F

FISH

YOUR FINGERS ARE THE **FISH 'S** UPPER FIN — AND YOUR FINGER AND THUMB CIRCLE ITS EYE.

G

GUN

POINTING THE FINGER AND THUMB TO LOOK LIKE A **GUN.**

H

HORSE

THE TWO FINGERS POINTING AT AN ANGLE ARE A **HORSE'S** HEAD.

i

THE LITTLE FINGER IS
A SMALL i AND IT IS
MADE OUT OF **ICE.**

ICE

J

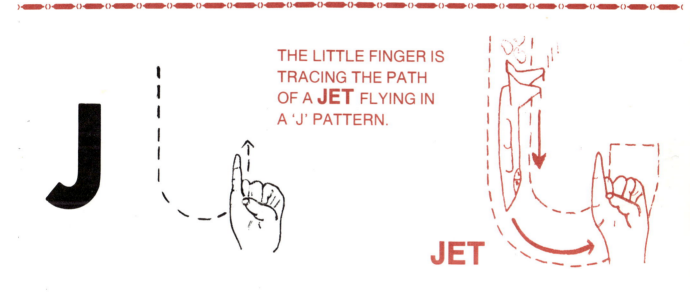

THE LITTLE FINGER IS
TRACING THE PATH
OF A **JET** FLYING IN
A 'J' PATTERN.

JET

K

KEY

THE TWO FINGERS
ARE MADE OF **KEYS**
AND THE THUMB
BETWEEN THEM IS A
KEY HOLE.

L

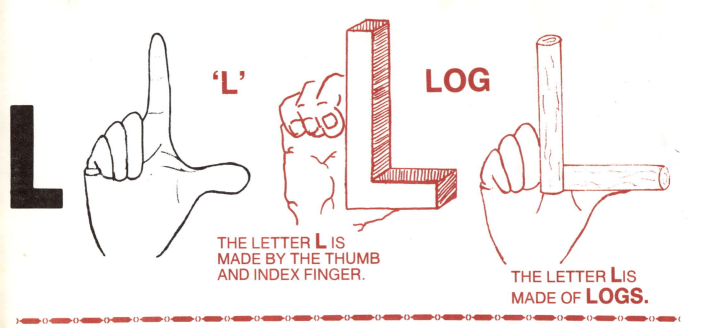

'L'

LOG

THE LETTER **L** IS MADE BY THE THUMB AND INDEX FINGER.

THE LETTER **L** IS MADE OF **LOGS.**

---

m

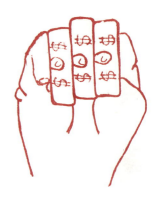

THREE FINGERS MAKE AN **'M'** BY HANGING OVER THE THUMB.

MONEY

THE **M** IS MADE OF **MONEY.**

---

n

 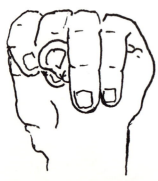

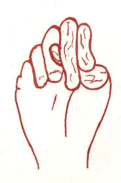

TWO FINGERS HANGING OVER THE THUMB MAKE THE **'N'.**

NUTS

THE **N** IS FULL OF **NUTS.**

O

OAK TREE

O

SEE THE OPENING IN THE **OAK TREE.**

P

PENCIL

POINT ONE **PENCIL** OUT AND WRITE WITH THE OTHER TWO.

Q

QUARTER

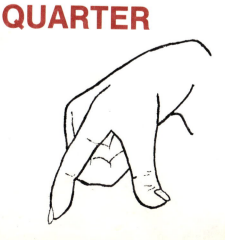

THE QUEEN IS PICKING UP A **QUARTER**

R

RABBIT

PICTURE A RABBIT WITH ITS EARS CROSSED.

S

SNAKE

SEE HOW THE HAND GRABS THE **SNAKE** IN A FIST.

T

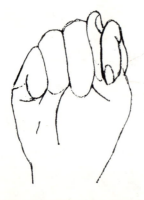

TEA

THE THUMB HAS BEEN REPLACED WITH A **TEA BAG** AND IS BEING SQUEEZED BY THE FINGERS.

U

UMBRELLA

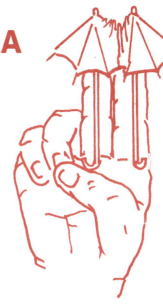

PICTURE TWO **UMBRELLAS** SMASHING TOGETHER.

V

TWO **VASES** ARE LEANING AWAY FROM EACH OTHER.

VASES

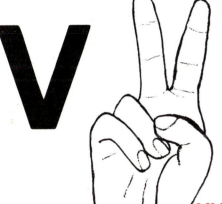

VICTORY

W

THREE WHISKEY BOTTLES — ONE IN THE MIDDLE AND TWO LEANING AWAY

WHISKEY

X

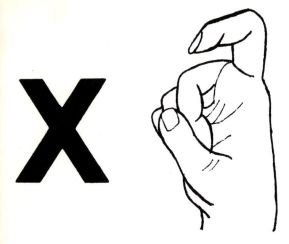

X-RAY

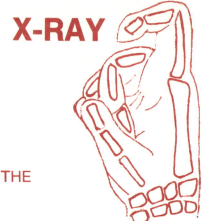

AN **X-RAY** OF THE CURVED INDEX FINGER.

Y

HOLDING TWO **YO-YOS** FAR APART WITH ONE HAND.

YO-YO

Z

ZEBRA

PAINTING A **Z** ON THE SIDE OF A **ZEBRA.**

(FOR THOSE WHO REMEMBER 'ZORRO' SLASHES A 'Z'.)

A   AN   HE   SHE   HER
HIM   HERS   HIS   THIS
THESE   THOSE   BY
OF   OR
THEIR   HI   AS   SO   EITHER

OTHER PRACTICE WORDS

VALENTINE, XEROX, WYOMING, PIZZA, CHICAGO, BIBLE,

QUACK, DICK JEFFERSON

PRACTICE PHRASES

SHE LIKES FRUIT   AN ELEPHANT

HE MARRIED HER   TEACH HIM THIS

THEIR CAT   A DRESS

A MEAL   SO IS HERS

SHE WAS BY HIM   THEY ATE

ZIP PANTS   EITHER THESE OR THOSE

GOOD AS HERS

TRY TO PRACTICE AT A MIRROR TO LEARN RECEPTION AND READING.

PRACTICE WITH A FRIEND.

HE

H   E

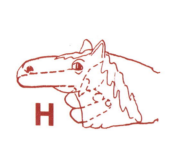 

H   E

THIS

T   H   I   S

T   H   I   S

OF

O   F

Introduction

We are pleased to present to you a newly developed and revolutionary memory aid designed specifically for students of signing.

'Word-picture association' has long been recognized as an important memory aid where people are able to increase mental storage with the help of a visual experience. By adapting this teaching technique to sign language, students learn at better than the normal pace.

This is accomplished by using an 'illogical picture association' memory process. Without realizing it, many people remember signs by associating them with pictures or actions that are produced in the mind. It is much easier to remember a picture than a word or even a hand motion. Many instructors already use a similar technique when they demonstrate a sign by showing its origin or by explaining the sign in such a manner that it builds a visual image in the mind.

This book produces those pictures for the student and does it in such a manner that the visual images are unforgettable. The memory experts who have written this book have gone to great lengths to design pictures and drawings that are unique enough to be committed to immediate memory.

Once the association between the sign, the sound-alike, and the picture is established, the student will retain the knowledge quickly and effectively. The logic behind the memory process. . . if you see a normal hand, you might not be able to remember it, but if you see a hand that is abnormal such as one that has a golf club for a finger you will never be able to forget it. The more abnormal the better you will remember it.

Instructor's Notes:

General Information—

As an instructor you have your own personality and teaching attitudes. These coupled with our memory system can produce a well-organized, very productive and enjoyable class.

Remind your students that there are several sign systems used throughout the country. Some signs may differ slightly from system to system, school to school and person to person. This book, however, is a basic communication process which will be easily understood by those who need an efficient introductory course.

Instructions for making the best use of this book:

It is important that the format for presentation of the signs to your class remain consistent. The total involvement of the participants is also necessary for a successful learning experience. The following format has been developed to give optimum class response:

It is assumed that all class members will have a text and are to be taught in order of presentation.

INSTRUCTOR
1. "The word is **WORK.** Watch me and make the sign for **WORK.**" (Instructor shows sign)
2. The word **WORK** sounds like **WORMS**—say work/**worms.**
3. "Look at the signture. **WORK/WORMS**—crushing the worms at the wrist." (Make sign while describing signture)
4. (Make the sign) and repeat, "Work/worm-crush the worms at the wrist-work/worm"
5. Show me the sign for work.
6. Introduce the next word.

STUDENT RESPONSE
1. Watch the instructor and imitate sign.
2. Repeat outloud, "**WORK** sounds like **WORMS**".
3. Look at the signture and repeat **WORK** sounds like **WORMS**—crushing worms at the wrist— make the sign.
4. Make the sign and repeat "**WORK/WORMS**" while looking away from the book and mentally picturing the signture drawing in the book.
5. Make the sign.
6. Watch Instructor.

Repeat this process through 9 word presentations. At the end review by the following method:

INSTRUCTOR
1. **CAN** sounds like   ?
2. "Show me the sign for **CAN.**
3. What is **the description?**

STUDENT
1. Say signture.
2. Show sign.
3. Describe signture.

At this point in the review the instructor should demonstrate the sign and require identification of the word from the student. At the end of each lesson sentences are provided and should be practiced by the students.

A review in the form of reading (from Instructor and other students) and signing expressively in phrases and sentences may be incorporated. Oral and manual participation by the class is essential.

Signing General Guidelines—
1. Always speak while signing;
2. Use good facial expression;
3. Sign smoothly and fluently;
4. Use correct signs--don't make up signs of your own.

LESSON 1

SOUNDS
LIKE . . .

NO

NOTE

CAN YOU CATCH A **NOTE** BETWEEN YOUR THUMB AND FINGERS?

CHANGE

SOUNDS
LIKE . . . **CHANGE**

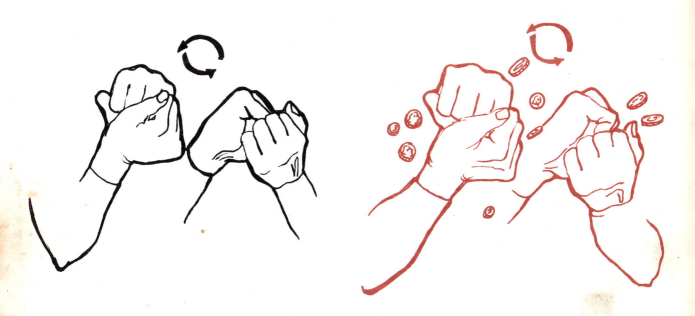

SEE THE PERSON WHO IS WRINGING **CHANGE** OUT OF HER HANDS.

SIGN

SOUNDS LIKE . . .

SIGN

PICTURE A POLICEMAN CIRCLING TWO **SIGNS** IN FRONT OF HIMSELF.

FINGERSPELL

SOUNDS LIKE . . .

FINGERSPELL

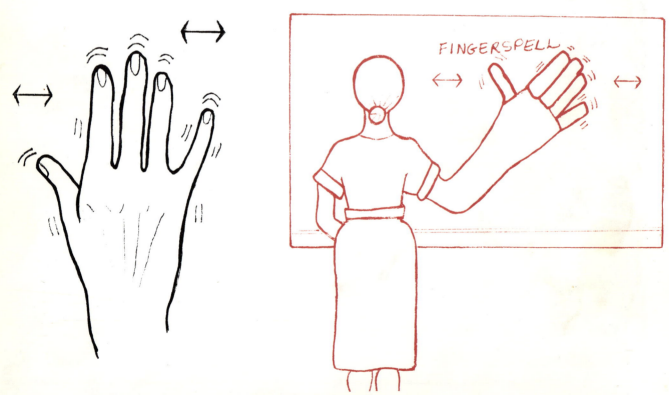

SEE THE TEACHER **FINGERSPELLING** LETTERS ON THE BLACKBOARD. ALL OF HER FINGERS HAVE TURNED TO CHALK.

WORD

SOUNDS LIKE . . .

WORD

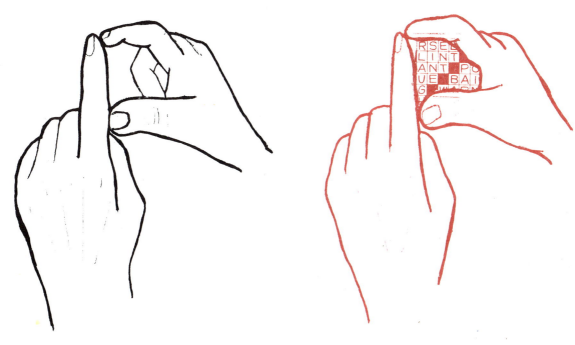

THE PERSON IS MAKING A WOODEN FRAME AROUND A **WORD PUZZLE.**

SOUNDS LIKE . . . **YOU**

YOU

YOUR COUNTRY WANTS **YOU!**

PERSON

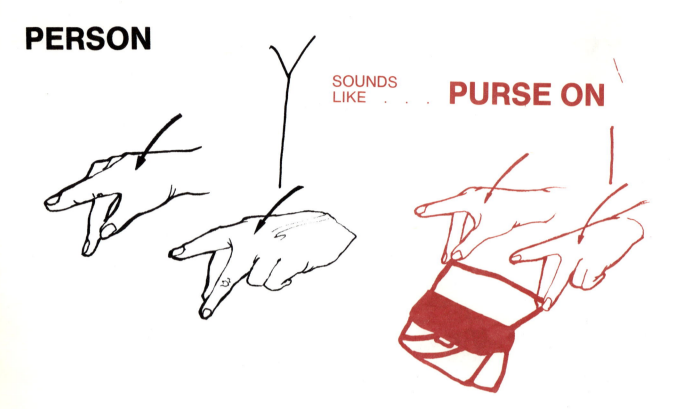

SOUNDS LIKE . . . **PURSE ON**

THE LADY IS PUTTING HER **PURSE ON** THE TABLE WITH THE LOWER FINGERS OF HER 'P' HANDS.

ME

SOUNDS LIKE . . . **ME**

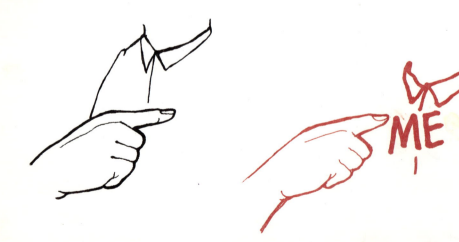

I WILL POINT TO **ME** WHEN I MEAN **ME**.

MY

SOUNDS LIKE . . . **MICE**

THE **MICE** ARE PULLED TOWARDS THE BODY.

（**MINE**）

SAME

SOUNDS LIKE . . . **SAM EGG**

SAM IS PUSHING HIS TWO **SAME** INDEX FINGERS INTO THE **SAME EGG.**

 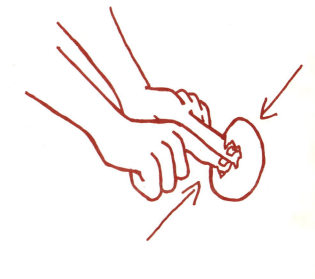

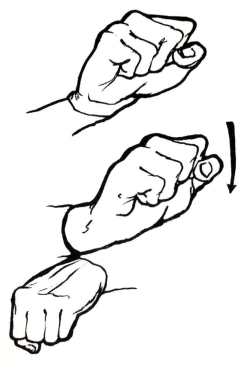

WORK

SOUNDS LIKE . . . **WORMS**

PICTURE A BOY SMASHING AND GRINDING **WORMS** BETWEEN HIS WRISTS.

GO

SOUNDS LIKE

GOPHER

PICTURE A PERSON PUSHING TWO **GO**PHERS AWAY WITH THE INDEX FINGERS.

COME

SOUNDS

LIKE . . .

COMPASS

COMPASS
SEE THE HUNTER
SPINNING A
COMPASS TOWARDS
HIS CHEST WITH
HIS INDEX FINGERS.

AM

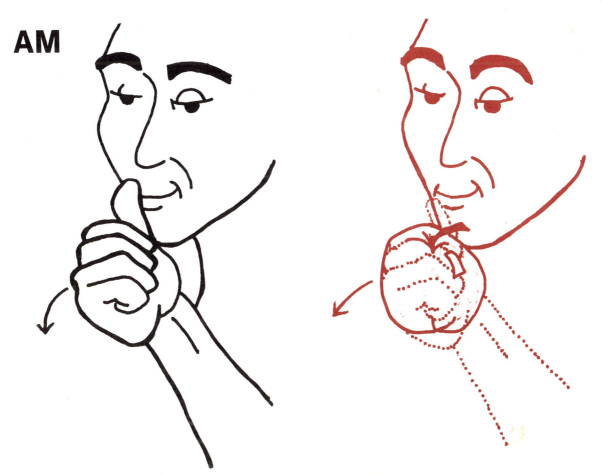

THE LETTER **A** LIKE IN **APPLE** IS COMING OFF OF THE CHIN.

IS

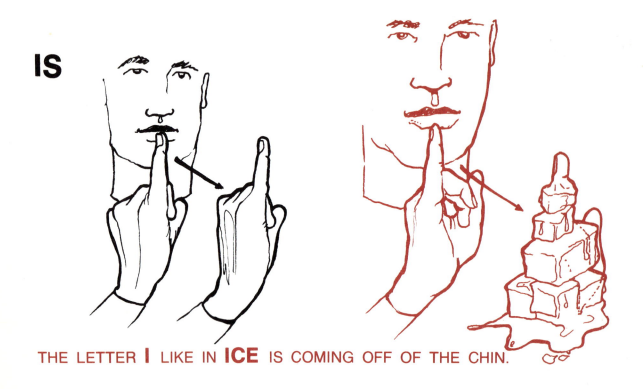

THE LETTER **I** LIKE IN **ICE** IS COMING OFF OF THE CHIN.

ARE

SOUNDS LIKE . . .

R

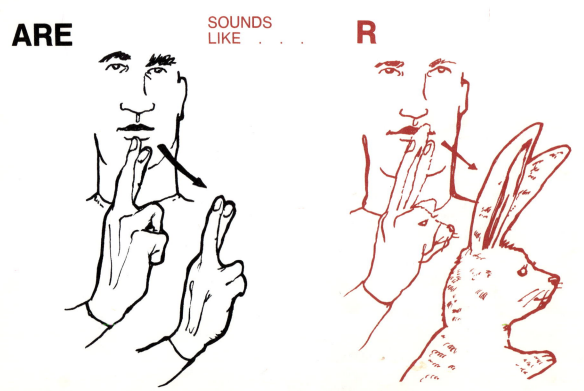

THE LETTER **R** LIKE IN **RABBIT** IS COMING OFF OF THE CHIN.

BE

THE LETTER **B**, AS IN BEES, IS COMING OFF OF THE CHIN.

I

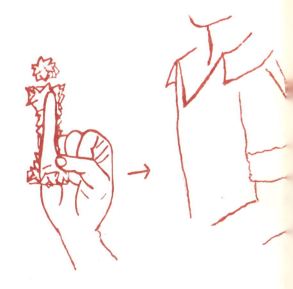

THE LETTER **I** AS IN ICE IS BROUGHT TOWARDS THE CHEST.

Test Yourself

_____sounds like_____and the sign is...

For example: CAN sounds like CANS. (Do the sign)

Use this review pattern for all words in this lesson and following lessons.

You have just memorized these signs:

same	**no**
word	**change**
go	**sign**
come	**fingerspell**
am	**work**
is	**you**
are	**person**
be	**me**
I	**my**

PRACTICE SENTENCES

(Spell the words that are underlined.)

1. <u>Max</u> is a <u>good</u> person.
2. Change <u>the</u> sign.
3. <u>Steve</u> <u>and</u> I are go<u>ing</u>.
4. Sign <u>the</u> word come.
5. <u>It</u> is <u>the</u> person I am.
6. My <u>answer</u> is no.
7. You <u>will</u> be <u>at</u> work.
8. Fingerspell me <u>the</u> same.
9. <u>Jessica</u> <u>will</u> be <u>there</u>.

YES　　SOUNDS LIKE . . .　　**YES**

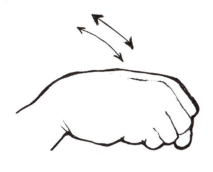

THE FIST HAS TURNED INTO A SMALL HEAD AND IS SHAKING ITS HEAD **YES, YES.**

IDEA　　SOUNDS LIKE . . .　　**IDEA**

AN **IDEA** IS COMING OUT OF THE BRAIN. A LIGHT BULB IS BALANCING ON THE LITTLE İ FINGER.

BOY

BOY SCOUT CAP

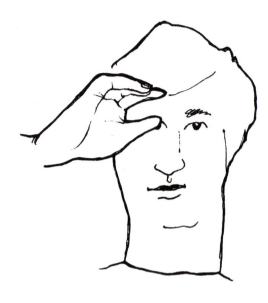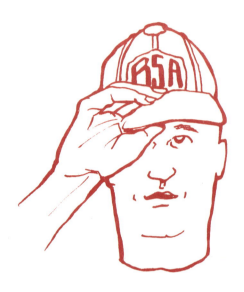

THE **BOY** SCOUT **IS** GRABBING THE BILL OF HIS **BOY** SCOUT CAP.

BROTHER — SIGN <u>BOY</u> AND <u>SAME</u>

GIRL

SOUNDS LIKE . . . **GIRDLE**

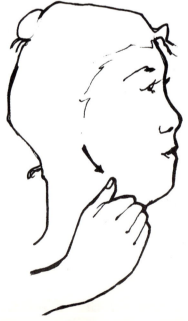

PICTURE A **GIRL** PULLING A GIRDLE OVER HER HEAD WITH HER THUMB.

SISTER — SIGN <u>GIRL</u> AND <u>SAME</u>

BABY

SOUNDS
LIKE . . .

BABY

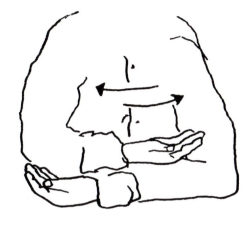

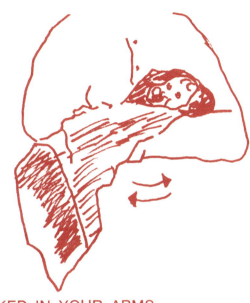

PICTURE A <u>BABY</u> BEING ROCKED IN YOUR ARMS.

WHAT

SOUNDS
LIKE . . . **WATT**

THE ONE HAND IS STRIKING AN ELECTRICAL **WATT SWITCH**
ON THE OTHER HAND.

WHEN

SOUNDS LIKE . . .

WHEN

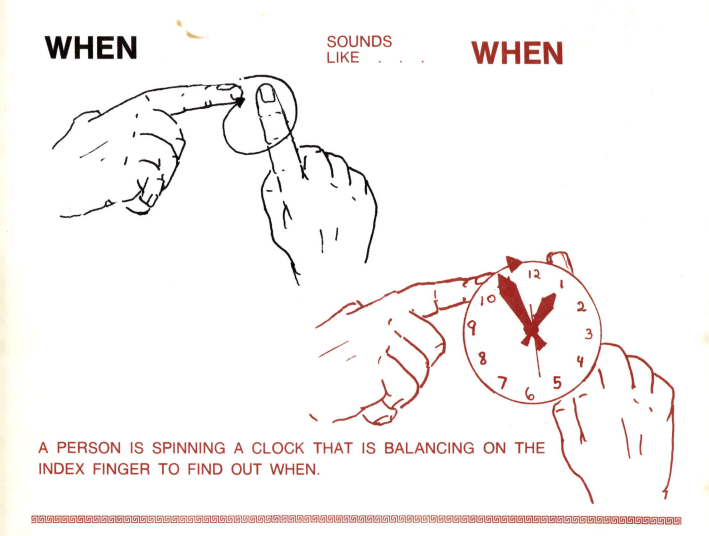

A PERSON IS SPINNING A CLOCK THAT IS BALANCING ON THE INDEX FINGER TO FIND OUT WHEN.

WHY

SOUNDS LIKE . . . **WIRE**

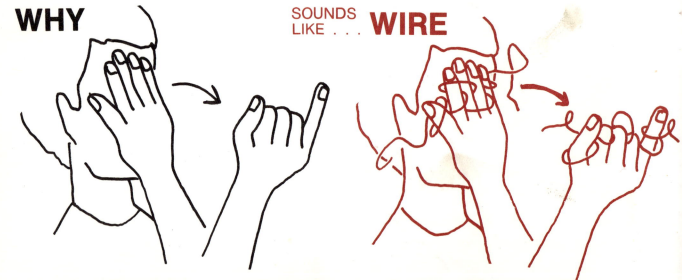

PICTURE THE LETTER 'Y' AS IN YO–YO S, PULLING **WIRES** OUT OF THE FOREHEAD.

WHERE

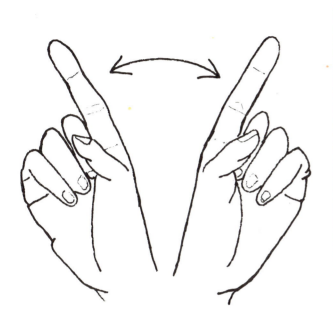

PICTURE A SMALL **WARE**HOUSE AND A PERSON WHO IS PUSHING THE SLIDING DOORS OPEN WITH THE INDEX FINGER. (SIDE TO SIDE).

HOW

SOUNDS LIKE . . . **HOE**

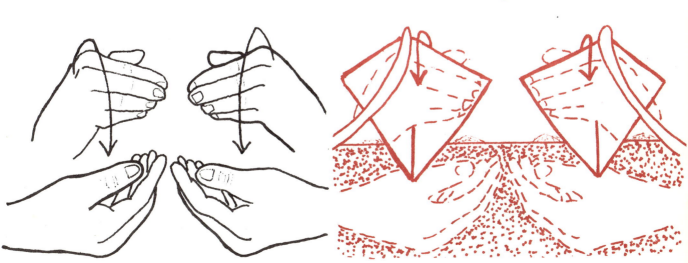

THE CUPPED HANDS ARE TWO **HOES** THAT ARE **HOEING** IN FRONT OF THE CHEST.

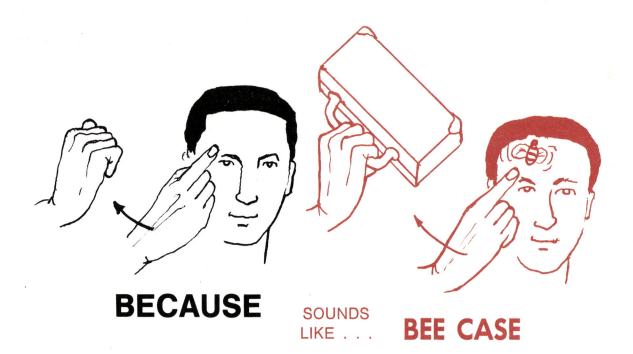

BECAUSE

SOUNDS
LIKE . . .   **BEE CASE**

PICTURE A BUSINESSMAN TOUCHING A BEE ON HIS FOREHEAD
AND THEN HOLDING A CASE UP IN THE AIR WITH A CLOSED FIST.

PICTURE A
HULA GIRL **WHO**
IS TWIRLING
HULAHOOPS
WITH HER
INDEX FINGER
AROUND HER
MOUTH.

WHO

SOUNDS
LIKE
HULA HOOP

WE

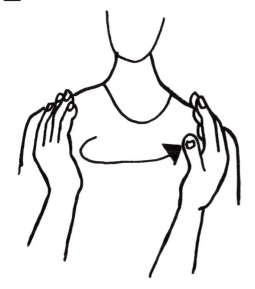

WE, US, OUR

A **WEASEL** IS HANGING OVER THE LADIES SHOULDER AND HER HAND IS SWEEPING ACROSS ITS BACK LIKE SHE IS PETTING THE **WEASEL**.

FOR

PICTURE A GOLFER HITTING A BALL OFF THE SIDE OF HIS HEAD. SAYING **FORE** AS HE SWINGS.

FOR   SOUNDS LIKE . . .   **FORE!**

CAN SOUNDS LIKE . . . **CANS**

 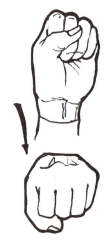  

TWO **CANS** ARE SITTING IN FRONT AND
BOTH ARE SMASHED AT THE SAME TIME WITH THE FISTS.

IT SOUNDS LIKE . . . **ITCHING POWDER**

IF THERE WERE **ITCHING POWDER** IN THE PALM OF THE
LEFT HAND YOU WOULD POKE IT WITH THE ITTY BITTY FINGER OF
THE OTHER.

THE

SOUNDS LIKE . . . **TUGGING 'T'**

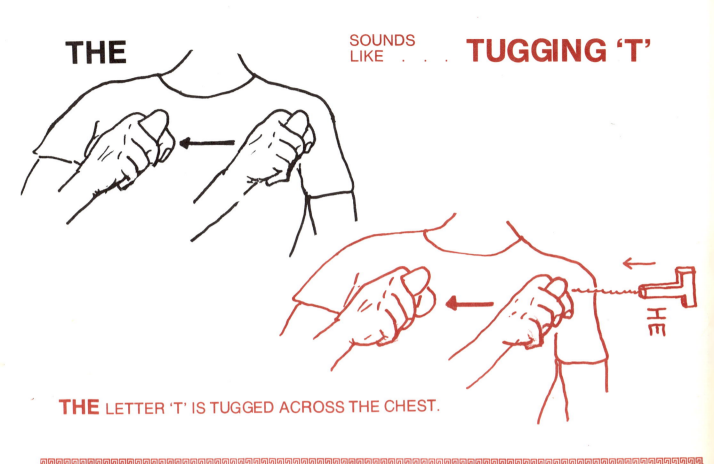

THE LETTER 'T' IS TUGGED ACROSS THE CHEST.

RIGHT

SOUNDS LIKE . . .

RIFLE

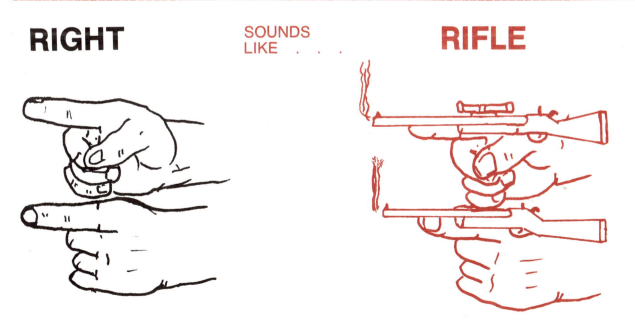

SEE THE TWO **RIFLES,** ONE ON TOP OF THE OTHER, SHOOTING AWAY FROM THE CHEST.

You have just memorized these signs:

Yes	how
idea	because
boy	who
girl	we
baby	for
what	can
when	it
why	the
where	right

PRACTICE SENTENCES

(Spell the words that are underlined.)

1. The boy is a baby.
2. What is the idea?
3. You can sign it right.
4. How is my girl?
5. We <u>say</u> yes because it is <u>good</u>.
6. I am working for you.
7. Why is it the same?
8. How can you fingerspell the word?
9. Who is the person?
10. Where <u>and</u> when can I work?

LESSON 3

KEY   SOUNDS LIKE . . .   **KEY**

IF YOUR LEFT HAND WAS A LOCK YOU WOULD TURN YOUR **KEY** IN IT.

TEACHER   SOUNDS LIKE . . .   **TEACHER**

THE **TEACHER** IS PULLING A BLACKBOARD OUT OF HER HEAD —THEN STANDING IT UP SO YOU CAN SEE IT.

MOTHER

SOUNDS
LIKE . . . **MOTHER GOOSE**

THE **MOTHER GOOSE** IS PECKING ON THE **MOTHER'S** CHIN

FATHER

SOUNDS
LIKE . . . **FEATHER**

THE HAND HAS TURNED TO **FEATHERS** AND THE THUMB **FEATHER** IS TICKLING THE **FATHER'S** FOREHEAD.

DOCTOR

SOUNDS LIKE . . . **DOCTOR**

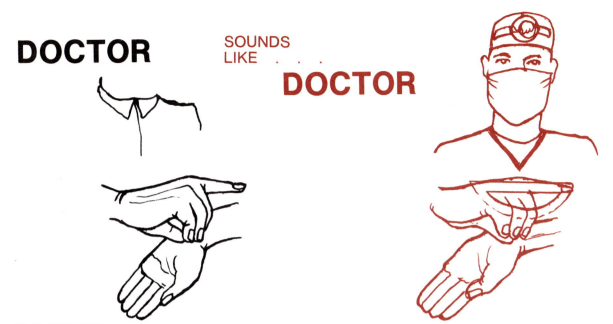

THE **DOCTOR** IS TAKING YOUR PULSE ON YOUR WRIST WITH THE LETTER 'D' HAND.

NURSE

SOUNDS LIKE . . . **NURSE**

THE **NURSE** IS TAKING YOUR PULSE .

HOSPITAL

SOUNDS LIKE . . .

HOSPITAL

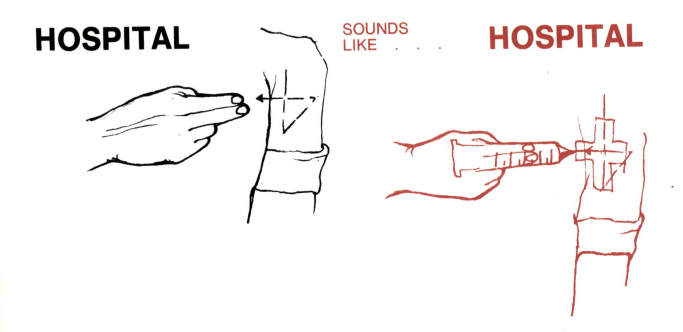

A RED CROSS IS DRAWN ON THE SHOULDER WITH A SYRINGE.
THE SYRINGE IS THE LETTER 'H' HAND.

DENTIST

SOUNDS LIKE . . .

DENTIST

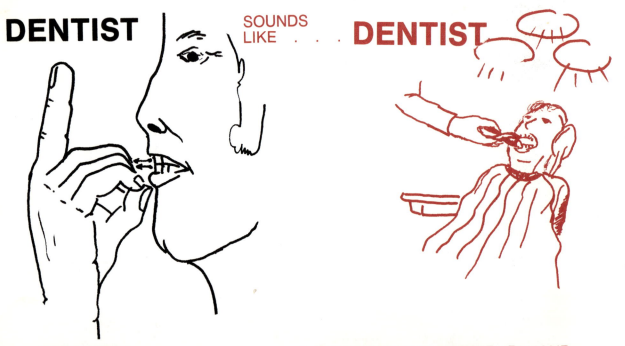

THE **DENTIST** IS PULLING YOUR TEETH OUT WITH THE LETTER 'D' HAND.

READ

SOUNDS LIKE . . . **READ**

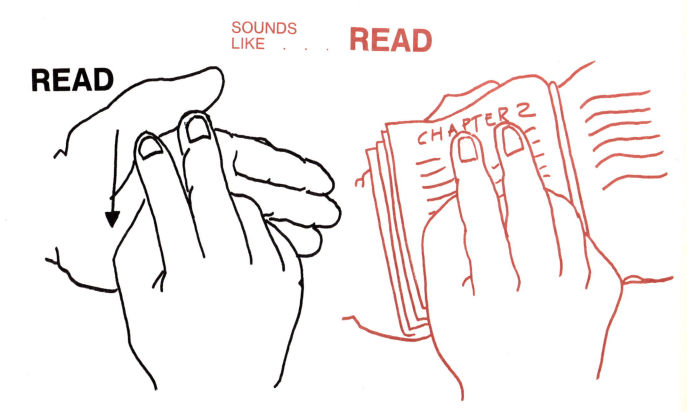

WHILE YOU ARE HOLDING A BOOK IN ONE HAND YOU WILL **READ** BY KEEPING TRACK WITH YOUR FINGERS.

WRITE

SOUNDS LIKE . . . **WRITE**

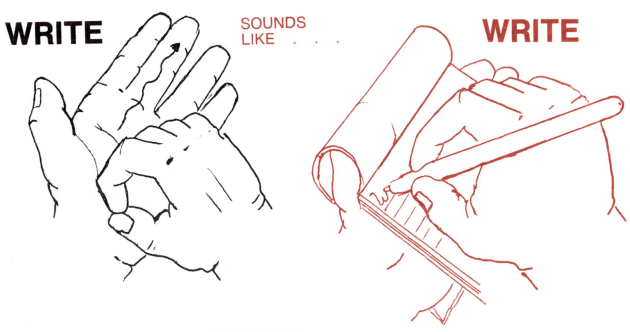

IF YOU HELD A **WRITING** PAD IN ONE HAND YOU WOULD **WRITE** ON IT WITH THE OTHER.

BOOK

SOUNDS
LIKE . . .

BOOK

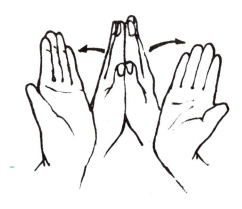
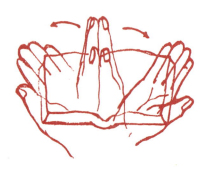

YOUR HANDS ARE OPENING AND HOLDING A **BOOK.**

PAPER

SOUNDS
LIKE . . .

PAPER

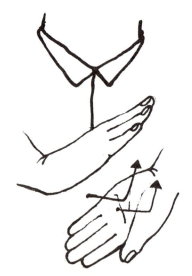

A **PAPER** IS BEING CRUMPLED BETWEEN THE PALMS OF THE HANDS; IT IS CRUNCHED TWICE.

NAME

SOUNDS
LIKE . . .

NAME

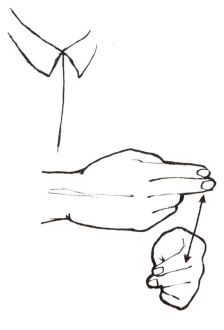

SEE THE PERSON HOLDING A **NAME** PLATE WITH TWO FINGERS OF EACH HAND.

COLD

SOUNDS
LIKE . . .

COLD

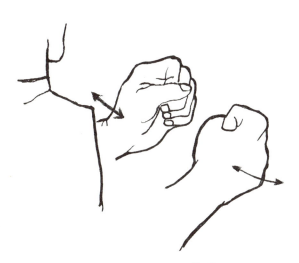

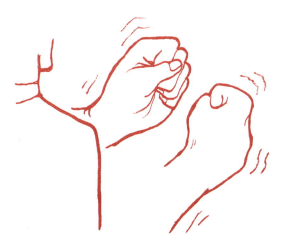

IF YOU WERE **COLD** YOU WOULD TIGHTEN YOUR FISTS AND "SHIVER" BACK AND FORTH.

SEE

SOUNDS LIKE . . . **SEE**

YOU CAN **SEE** BETTER IF YOU MOVE YOUR EYES CLOSER. YOU CAN BALANCE THEM ON YOUR FINGERS.

STAND

SOUNDS LIKE . . . **STAND**

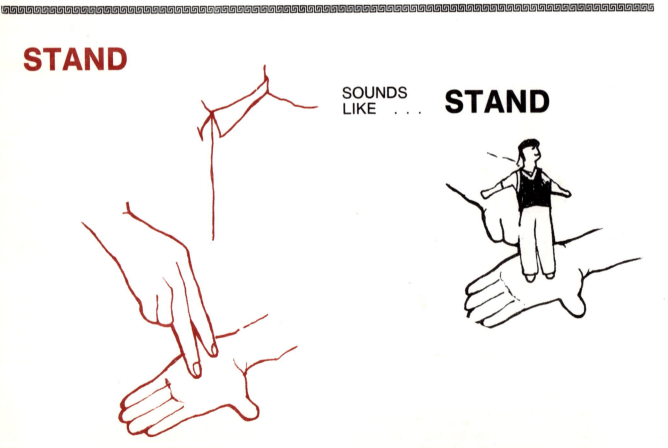

THE BOY IS **STAND**ING IN THE HAND—HIS LEGS ARE FINGERS.

HAVE

SOUNDS LIKE . . . **HALF**

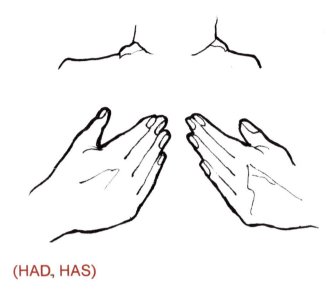 

(HAD, HAS)

THE MAN WILL **HAVE** TO TOUCH HIMSELF ON HIS CHEST WITH BOTH HANDS TO SPLIT HIS BODY IN **HALF.**

MEET

SOUNDS LIKE . . . **MEAT**

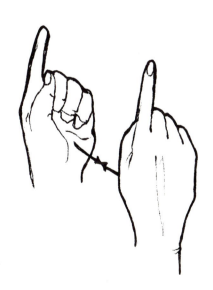 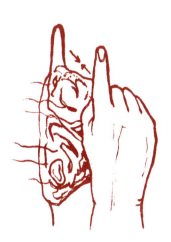

BOTH INDEX FINGERS POINT UP AND **MEET** TOGETHER IN FRONT TO PRESS SOME **MEAT.**

You have just memorized these signs:

mother	paper
father	hospital
doctor	dentist
nurse	name
key	cold
teacher	see
read	stand
write	have
book	meet

PRACTICE SENTENCES
(Spell the words that are underlined.)

1. My father is a doctor.
2. My mother is a teacher.
3. The nurse can read.
4. I have a book to work on.
5. I can see the hospital <u>if</u> I stand.
6. It is <u>too</u> cold to write.
7. I can meet the person.
8. Write the name <u>on</u> the paper.
9. What is the name of the boy?
10. My key is for you.

NEW

SOUNDS LIKE . . . **NEW YORK**

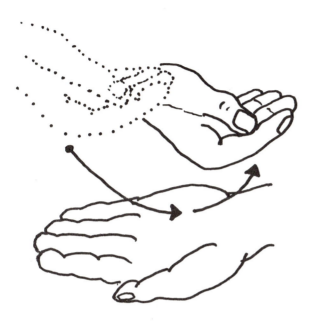

SEE THE CITY OF **NEW** YORK SCOOPED OUT OF THE LEFT HAND.

BREAKFAST

SOUNDS LIKE . . . **BREAKFAST**

THE 'B' HAND IS AT THE MOUTH EATING **BREAKFAST.**

LUNCH

SOUNDS LIKE . . . **LUNCH**

THE 'L' LETTER IS AT THE MOUTH EATING **LUNCH.**

DINNER

SOUNDS LIKE . . . **DINNER**

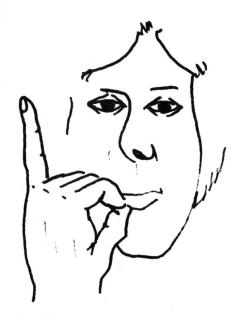 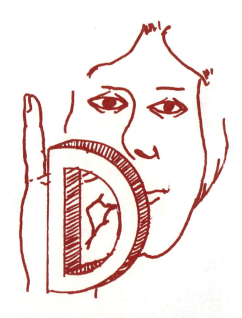

THE 'D' LETTER IS AT THE MOUTH EATING **DINNER.**

EAT

SOUNDS LIKE . . .

EAT

PICTURE A PERSON PUTTING EEL MEAT TO HIS MOUTH AND **EATING** IT.

DRINK

SOUNDS LIKE . . .

DRINK

YOU CAN **DRINK** EVERY DROP OUT OF THE GLASS BY TURNING IT UP AT YOUR MOUTH.

FORK

SOUNDS LIKE . . . **FORK**

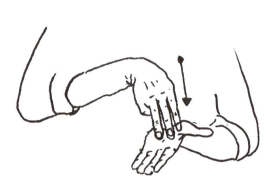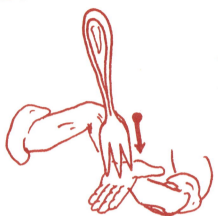

THE THREE FINGERS ARE THE TINES OF THE **FORK** POKING INTO THE OTHER PALM.

SPOON

SOUNDS LIKE . . . **SPOON**

SPOONING SOUP OUT OF THE OTHER HAND THAT HAS TURNED INTO A BOWL.

KNIFE

KNIFE

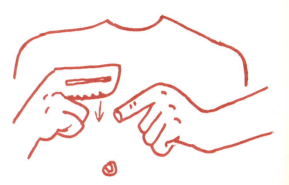

THE FINGER OF THE RIGHT HAND HAS CUT THE FINGER OF THE LEFT HAND IN HALF LIKE A **KNIFE.**

PLATE

PLATE

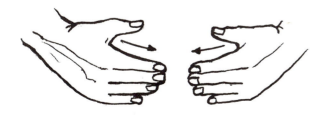

A **PLATE** IS HELD IN THE HANDS.

CUP

SOUNDS
LIKE . . .

CUP

A **CUP** IS HELD IN THE HAND.

GLASS

SOUNDS
LIKE . . .

GLASS

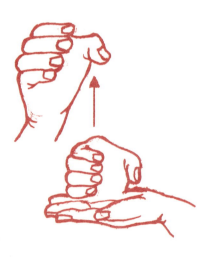

A TALL **GLASS** IS LIFTED OFF OF THE HAND.

BOWL

SOUNDS LIKE . . .

BOWL

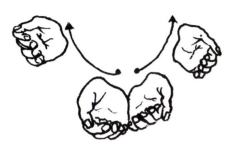

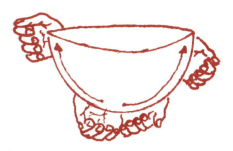

A **BOWL** IS SHAPED IN FRONT OF YOU.

TOILET

SOUNDS LIKE . . .

TOILET

THE LETTER 'T' IS MOVING TOWARDS THE **TOILET.**

MORE

SOUNDS LIKE . . . **MORSE CODE**

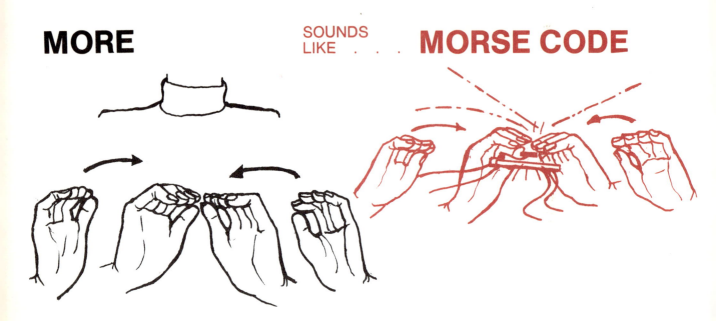

SEE THE PERSON TAPPING OUT **MORE MORSE** CODE.

GOOD

SOUNDS LIKE . . . **GOOSE**

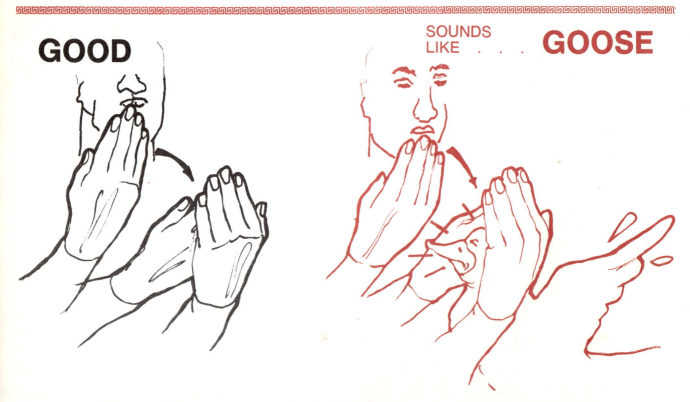

A PERSON IS BACKHANDING A **GOOSE** HEAD THAT IS IN THE OTHER UPRIGHT PALM.

BAD

SOUNDS LIKE . . . **BAT**

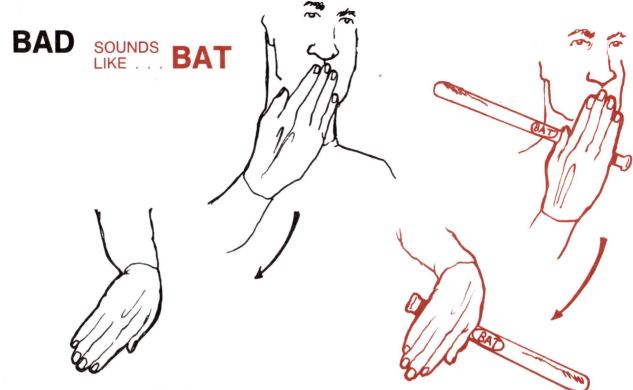

IT IS BEING **BATTED** AWAY FROM THE MOUTH BECAUSE IT IS **BAD.**

SCHOOL

SOUNDS LIKE . . .

SCHOOL

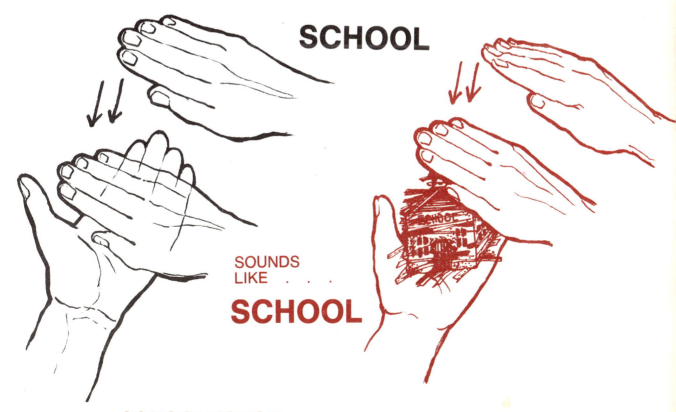

THE **SCHOOLHOUSE** IS BEING PRESSED BETWEEN THE PALMS OF THE HANDS.   IT IS CRUNCHED TWICE.

You have just memorized these signs:

new	plate
breakfast	cup
lunch	glass
dinner	bowl
eat	toilet
drink	more
fork	good
spoon	bad
knife	school

PRACTICE SENTENCES
(Spell the words that are underlined.)

1. The idea is new.
2. My teacher is <u>at</u> school.
3. The boy <u>will</u> eat a good lunch.
4. What <u>do</u> you drink for breakfast?
5. You can drink more <u>from</u> a glass.
6. The nurse <u>said</u> the dinner is bad.
7. It is my plate and cup.
8. The girl <u>put</u> the spoon <u>in</u> the bowl.
9. Can you <u>cut</u> with a fork?
10. Why <u>did</u> the doctor <u>use</u> the knife?

GIVE

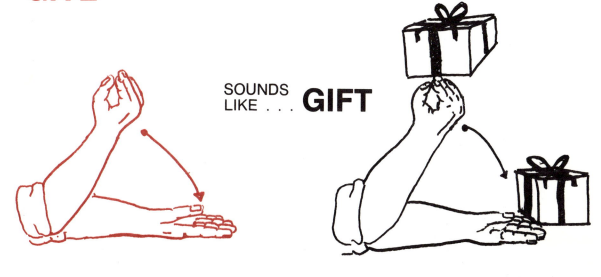

SOUNDS LIKE . . . **GIFT**

PRESENTING A **GIFT** TO SOMEONE.

BUT

SOUNDS LIKE . . . **BUTT**

PICTURE A PERSON MAKING TWO CIRCLES OUT OF CIGARETTE **BUTTS.**

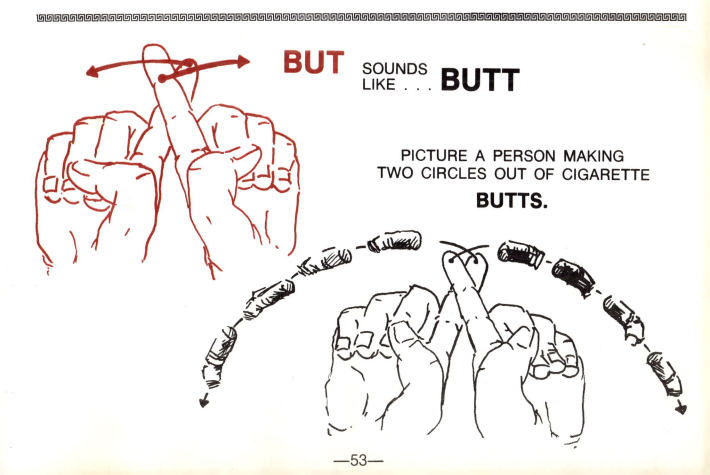

TAKE

SOUNDS LIKE . . .

TAKE

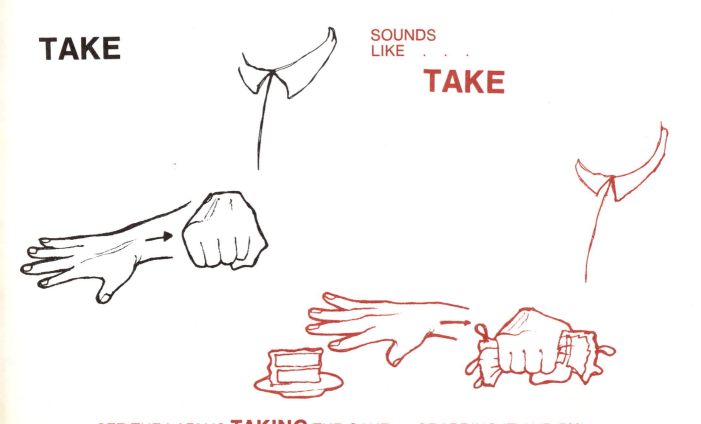

SEE THE LADY IS **TAKING** THE CAKE — GRABBING IT AND PULLING IT TOWARD HER.

WALK

SOUNDS LIKE . . . **WALK**ING

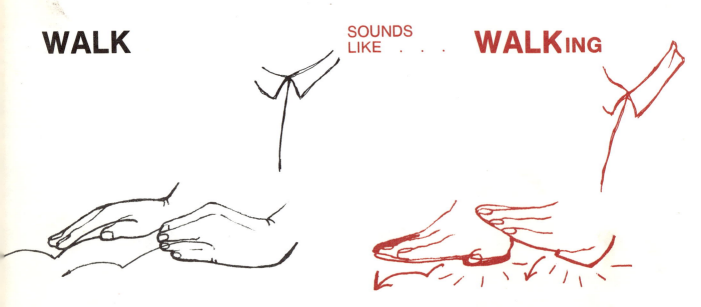

THE HANDS ARE SHOES AND THEY ARE **WALKING.**

AND

SOUNDS LIKE . . . **ANT**

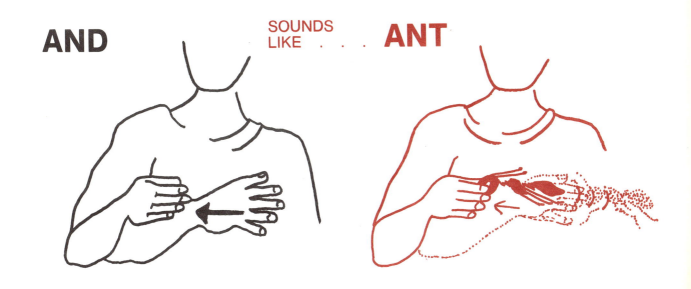

THE RIGHT HAND IS GRABBING THE HEAD OF A LARGE **ANT** AND PULLING IT ACROSS THE CHEST.

KIND

SOUNDS LIKE . . . **KITE**

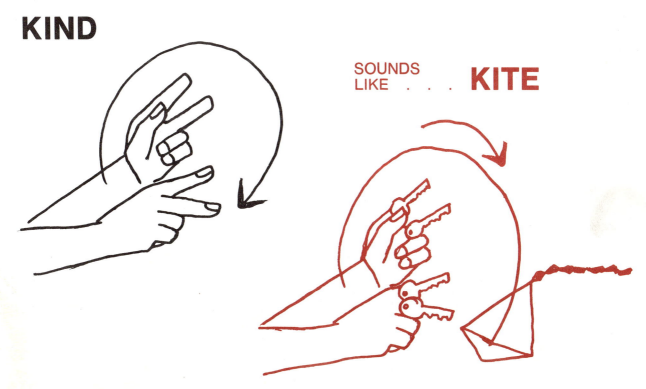

THE LETTER 'K' HANDS POINT OUT FRONT AND THEN THE RIGHT IS PULLED OVER THE LEFT BY A **KITE.**

TO

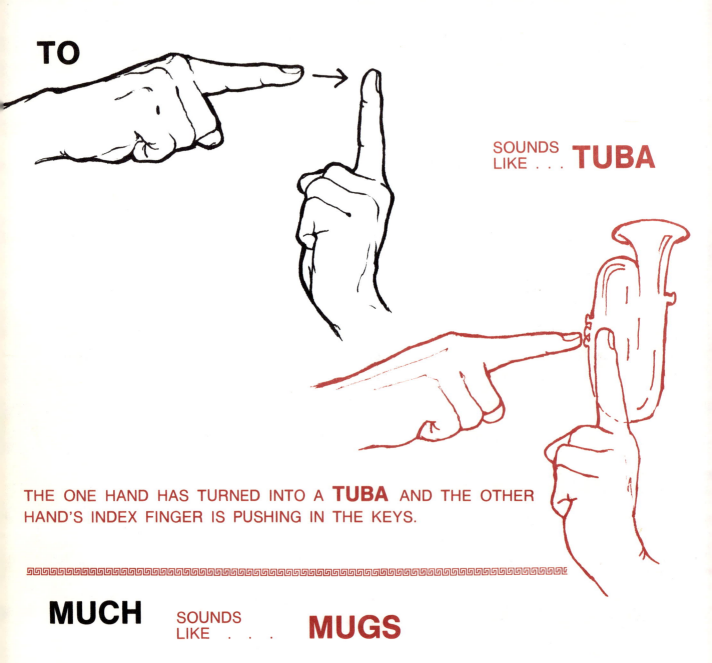

SOUNDS LIKE . . . **TUBA**

THE ONE HAND HAS TURNED INTO A **TUBA** AND THE OTHER HAND'S INDEX FINGER IS PUSHING IN THE KEYS.

MUCH   SOUNDS LIKE . . .   MUGS

YOU ARE HOLDING TWO **MUGS** BY THE HANDLES THAT ARE TOASTING EACH OTHER AND THEN PULLING BACK.

GET

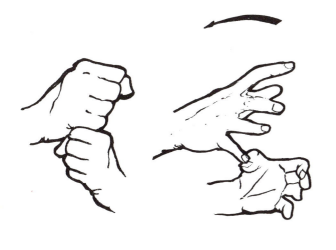

SOUNDS LIKE ... **GOAT**

THE PERSON IS REACHING OUT AND **GETTING** A **GOAT** AROUND ITS NECK.

UNDER

SOUNDS LIKE ... **UNDERLINE**

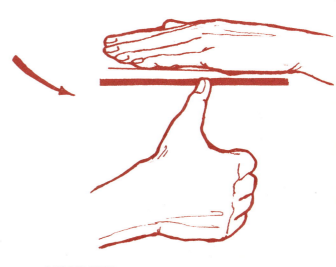

THE THUMB IS DRAWING A LINE **UNDER** THE OTHER OPEN HAND.

SANDWICH

SOUNDS
LIKE . . .

SANDWICH

THE HANDS HAVE TURNED TO BREAD AND MAKE A **SANDWICH** THAT YOU CAN PUT TO YOUR MOUTH.

COFFEE

SOUNDS
LIKE . . .

COFFEE

THE HANDS HAVE TURNED INTO **COFFEE** GRINDERS.

WATER

SOUNDS LIKE . . .

WATER

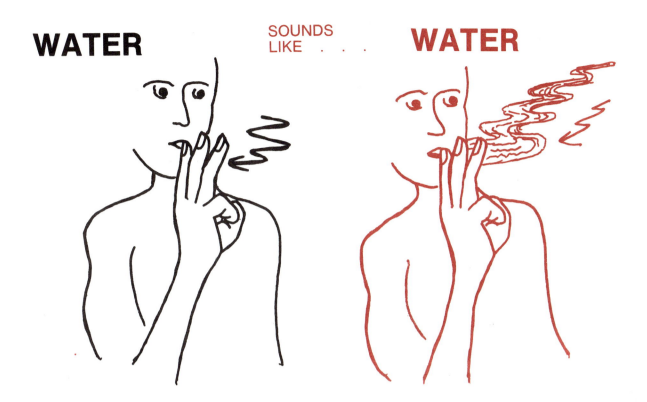

THE 'W' LETTER IS FOLLOWING A RIVER OF **WATER** INTO THE MOUTH.

MILK

SOUNDS LIKE . . .

MILK

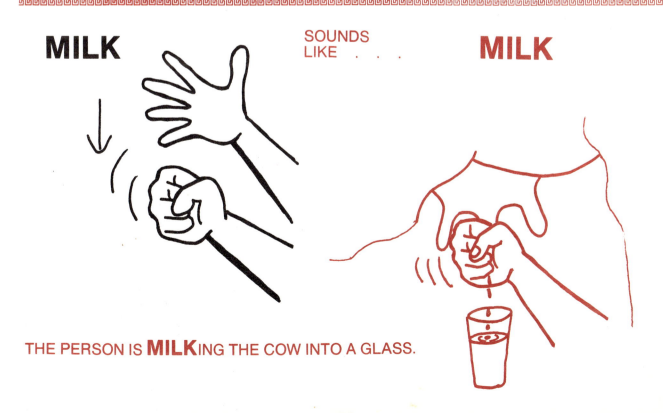

THE PERSON IS **MILK**ING THE COW INTO A GLASS.

TABLE

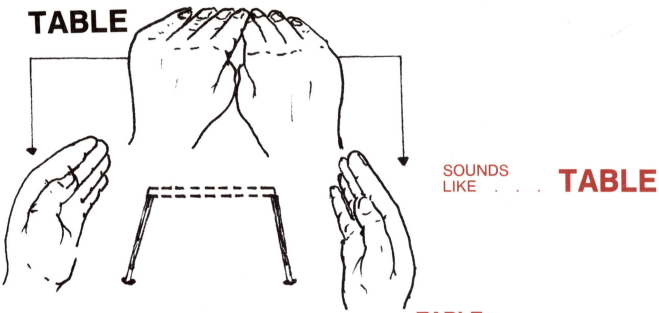

SOUNDS LIKE . . . **TABLE**

THE HANDS ARE RUBBING THE TOP OF THE **TABLE,** THEN GOING ON DOWN THE LEGS.

(DESK)

WRONG

SOUNDS LIKE . . . **ROCK**

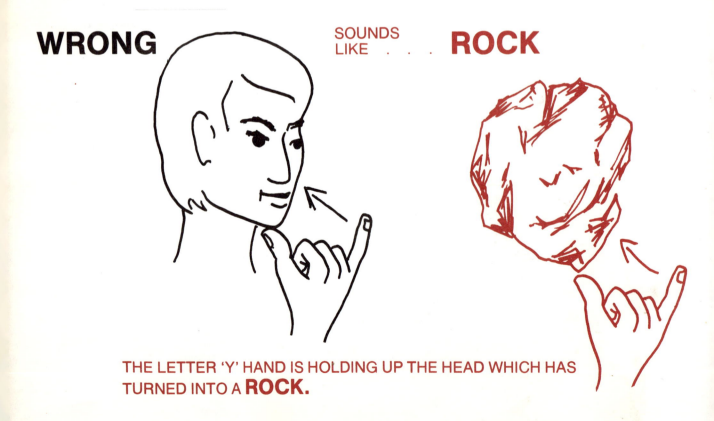

THE LETTER 'Y' HAND IS HOLDING UP THE HEAD WHICH HAS TURNED INTO A **ROCK.**

CHILDREN

SOUNDS
LIKE . . .

CHILDREN

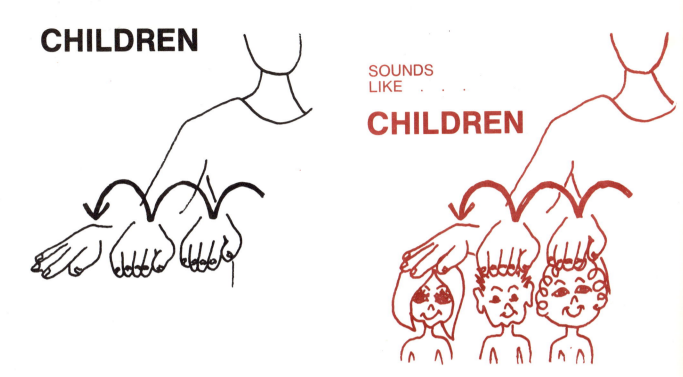

THE PARENT IS PATTING THE **CHILDREN** ON THE HEAD.

FROM

SOUNDS
LIKE . . . **FROG**

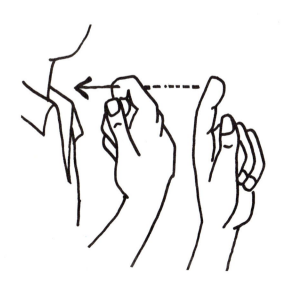

THE **FROG** IS JUMPING FROM THE INDEX FINGER OF THE LEFT
HAND TO THE PERSON'S NECK.

You have just memorized these signs:

under	give
sandwich	but
coffee	take
water	walk
milk	and
table	kind
children	to
from	much
wrong	get

PRACTICE SENTENCES

(Spell the words that are underlined.)

1. Where <u>did</u> you get <u>that</u> sandwich?
2. How much is the coffee?
3. It is wrong to take milk from the children.
4. My father can walk to school.
5. It is under the table.
6. Give the teacher <u>some</u> water.
7. I <u>will</u> go, but <u>not</u> to work.
8. What kind <u>of</u> person are you?
9. The boy and girl are bad.
10. My coffee is <u>too</u> cold <u>to</u> drink.

THANK

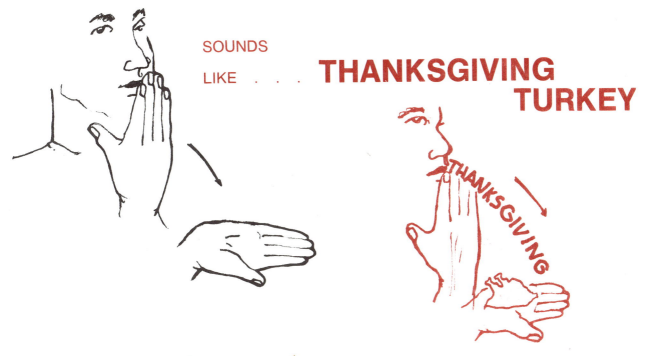

SOUNDS LIKE . . .

THANKSGIVING TURKEY

TAKING A **THANKS**GIVING TURKEY OUT OF THE MOUTH AND HOLDING IT OUT IN YOUR HAND.

PAY

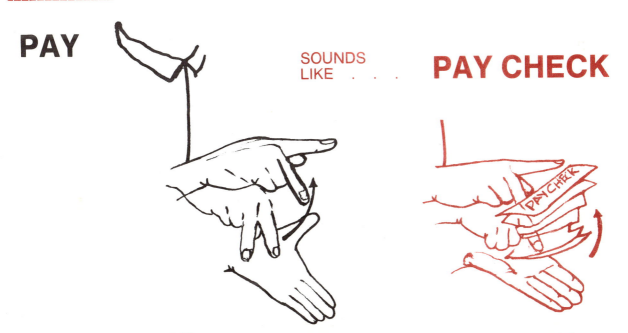

SOUNDS LIKE . . .

PAY CHECK

A PILE OF **PAY**CHECKS IN THE PALM IS BEING SNAPPED UP INTO THE AIR.

YOUR

SOUNDS LIKE . . . **YAWN**

YOUR HAND IS COVERING THE <u>YAWN</u>ING MOUTH OF A FLOATING HEAD.

WAIT

SOUNDS LIKE . . . **WEIGHT**

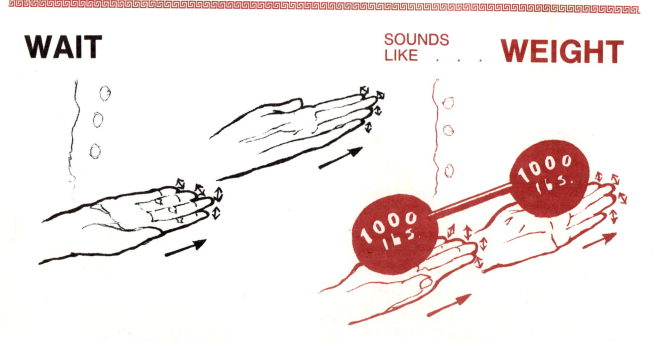

THE HANDS ARE HOLDING UP A LOT OF **WEIGHT.**

CLOTHING

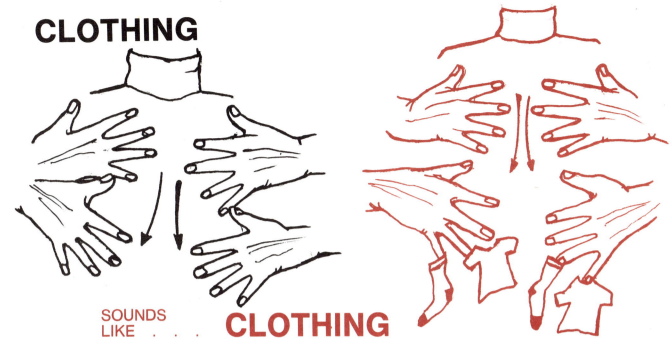

SOUNDS LIKE . . . **CLOTHING**

A SHIRT THAT IS BEING PUSHED DOWN IS IMPRINTED WITH ALL KINDS OF <u>CLOTHING</u>—SOCKS, SHIRTS, PANTS, **DRESSES.**

(DRESS)

COAT

SOUNDS LIKE . . .

COAT

THE LADY IS PULLING A MINK **COAT** OVER HER SHOULDERS.

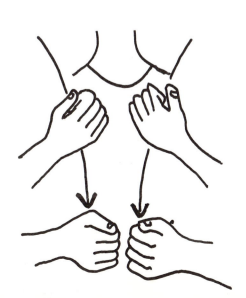

PANTS

SOUNDS LIKE . . .

PANTS

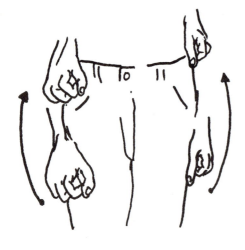 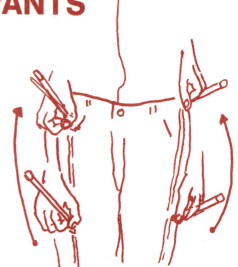

THE MAN IS DRAWING A STRIPE UP THE SIDE OF HIS **PANTS.**

SHOES

SOUNDS LIKE . . .

SHOES

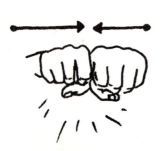 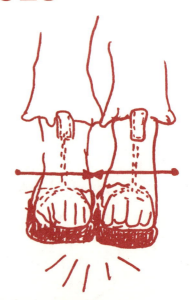

SEE THE SOLDIER CLICKING THE HEELS OF HIS **SHOES.** THE FISTS ARE THE HEELS.

SHOWER

SOUNDS LIKE . . .

SHOWER

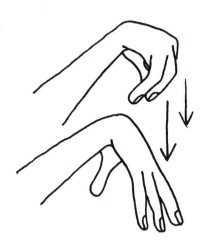

THE HAND IS A **SHOWER** HEAD SPRAYING WATER OVER THE HEAD.

WASH

SOUNDS LIKE . . .

WASH

THE LADY IS **WASHING** CLOTHES BY RUBBING THEM TOGETHER.

SOAP

SOUNDS
LIKE . . .

SOAP

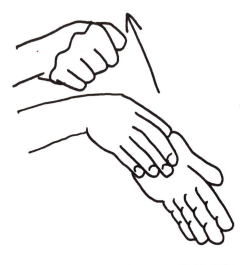

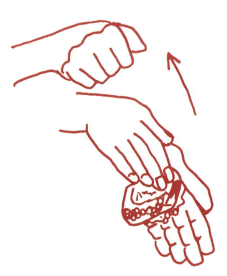

RUBBING THE **SOAP** BETWEEN THE HANDS.

FIRE

SOUNDS
LIKE . . .

FIRE

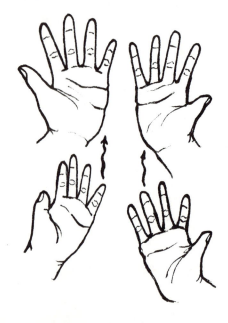

THE **FIRE** FLAMES ARE BURNING UP.

TELEPHONE

SOUNDS LIKE . . . **TELEPHONE**

YOUR RIGHT HAND IS IMITATING A **TELEPHONE** HANDLE AND YOU ARE HOLDING IT TO YOUR HEAD.

TIME

SOUNDS LIKE . . . **TIME PIECE**

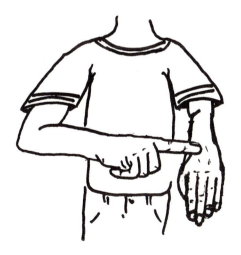
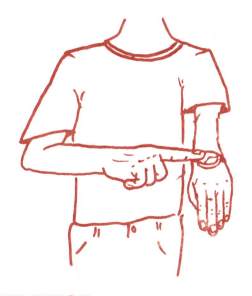

POINT TO THE WATCH WHICH IS A **TIME PIECE** ON YOUR LEFT WRIST TO TELL **TIME.**

HELP

SOUNDS LIKE . . . **HELICOPTER**

THE LEFT FIST HAS CHANGED TO A HELICOPTER AND IS **HELPED** UP BY THE RIGHT PALM.

MAKE

SOUNDS LIKE . . . **MAKE UP**

THE LADY IS SMASHING HER **MAKE** UP BETWEEN HER FISTS.

SOME

SOUNDS LIKE . . . **SUMMER SAUSAGE**

THE LEFT HAD HAS TURNED INTO A LINK OF **SUMMER SAU-SAGE** AND THE RIGHT HAND IS LIKE A KNIFE CUTTING IT.

MYSELF

SOUNDS LIKE . . . **MICE ELF**

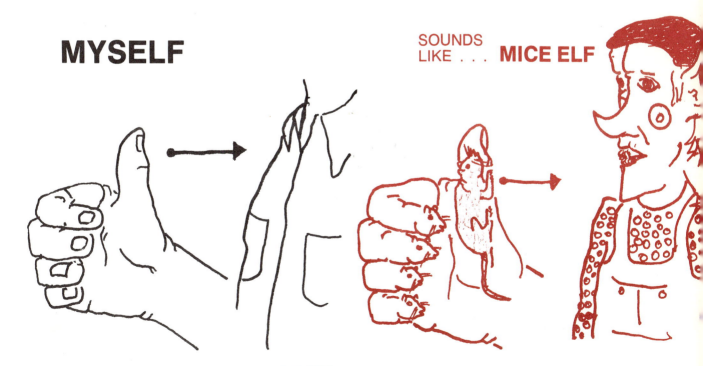

HIS HAND IS MADE OF **MICE** AND THE BIGGEST ONE, THAT IS THE THUMB, IS STICKING ITS HEAD UP AND THE **ELF** IS PULLING THE **MICE** TOWARDS HIS BODY.

You have just memorized these signs:

thank	wash
pay	soap
your	fire
wait	telephone
clothing	time
coat	help
pants	make
shoes	Some
shower	myself

PRACTICE SENTENCES

1. What time is your lunch?
2. How much can you pay for it?
3. I can wash the clothing myself.
4. Thank the boy for the shoes.
5. Wait for the teacher to help you.
6. Take your coat and pants to school.
7. Get some help for the fire.
8. Can your mother make soap?
9. The boy can take a shower.
10. My children have a telephone.

ON

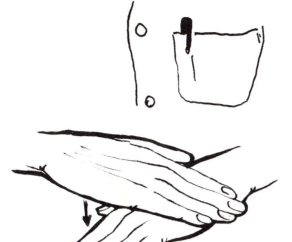

SOUNDS LIKE . . . **ONION**

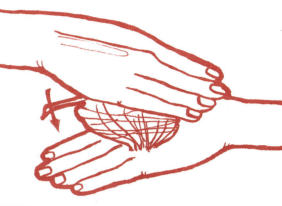

PICTURE A PERSON HOLDING AN **ONION** ON THE BACK OF ONE HAND AND PUSHING IT DOWN WITH THE OTHER.

HANDS <u>ON</u> TOP OF EACH OTHER

OFF

SOUNDS LIKE . . . **OFFICER**

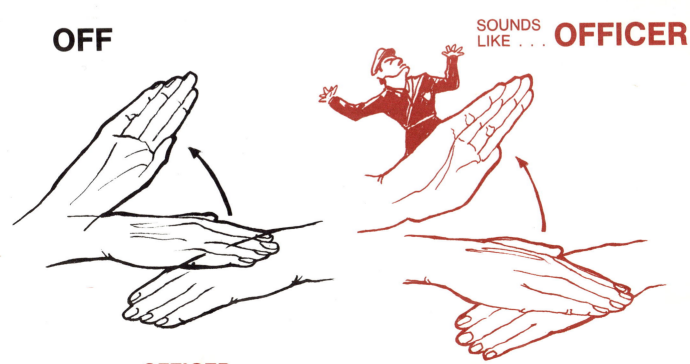

THE **OFFICER** THAT WAS STANDING ON BOTH HANDS IS NOW THROWN **OFF.**

LARGE, BIG

SOUNDS LIKE . . .

LARGE LOG

THE LOGGER STARTS OUT HOLDING A SMALL LOG ON HIS FINGERS & THUMB; THEN THE LOG GROWS **BIGGER** AND **LARGER.**

SMALL, LITTLE

SOUNDS LIKE . . .

SMALL LILY

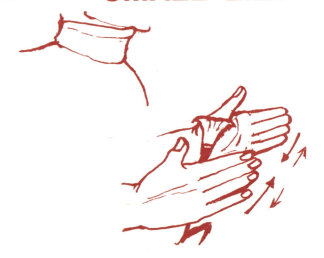

THE **SMALL** MAN IS SMASHING A **LITTLE** LILY IN FRONT OF THE CHEST.

OPEN

SOUNDS LIKE . . . **OPEN**

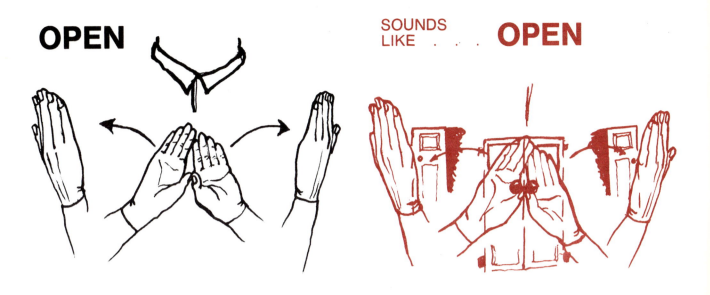

YOU HAVE **OPENED** YOUR HANDS WHICH ARE THE DOORS OF A MANSION.

CLOSE

SOUNDS LIKE . . . **CLOSE**

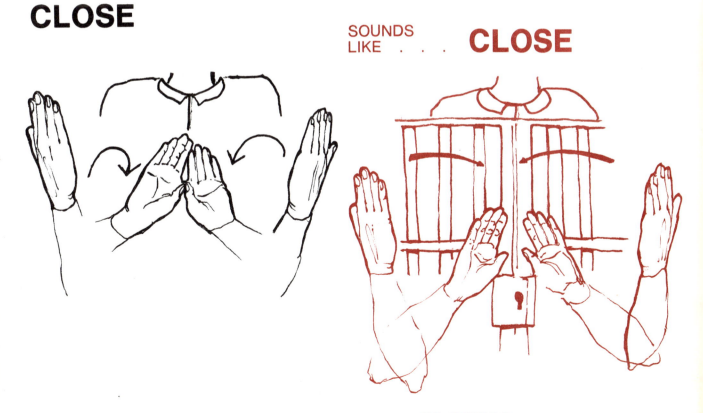

THE HANDS ARE JAIL DOORS AND ARE **CLOSING** YOU IN.

IN

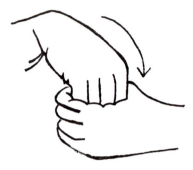

IF YOUR LEFT HAND WAS A BOTTLE OF **INK** WOULD YOU PUT YOUR HAND **IN** IT?

SOUNDS LIKE . . . **INK**

INK

OUT

SOUNDS LIKE . . . **OUTLAWS OUTBOARD MOTOR**

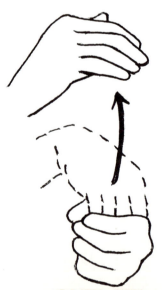

AN **OUTLAW** IS PULLING AN **OUTBOARD** MOTOR OUT OF HIS HAND.

UP

SOUNDS LIKE . . . **UP**

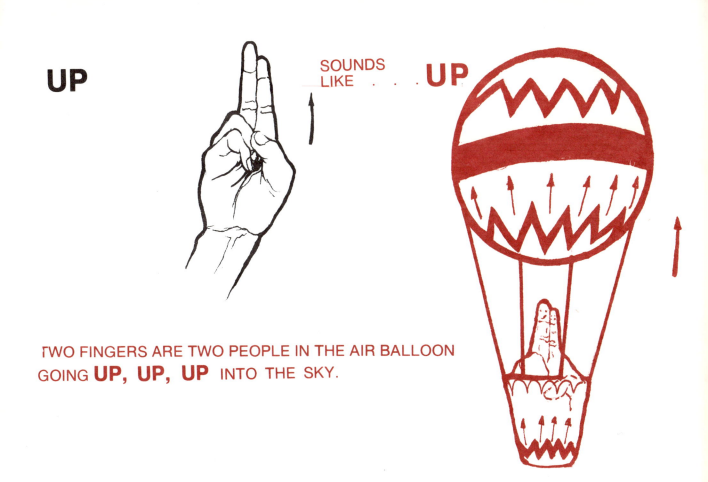

TWO FINGERS ARE TWO PEOPLE IN THE AIR BALLOON GOING **UP, UP, UP** INTO THE SKY.

DOWN

SOUNDS LIKE . . . **DOWN**

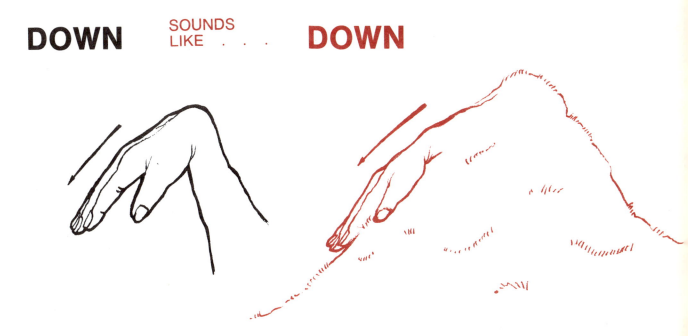

THE HAND IS GOING **DOWN, DOWN, DOWN** THE HILL.

WITH

SOUNDS LIKE . . . **WITCH**

A MEAN OLD **WITCH** IS BEING SMASHED BETWEEN THE FISTS.

TOGETHER

SOUNDS LIKE . . . **TO-GET-HER**

A LADY IS TRYING **TO-GET-HER** COAT OFF AND AWAY FROM HER BODY.

OVER

OVAL

MAKE AN **OVAL OVER** YOUR LEFT HAND WITH YOUR RIGHT.

FORGET

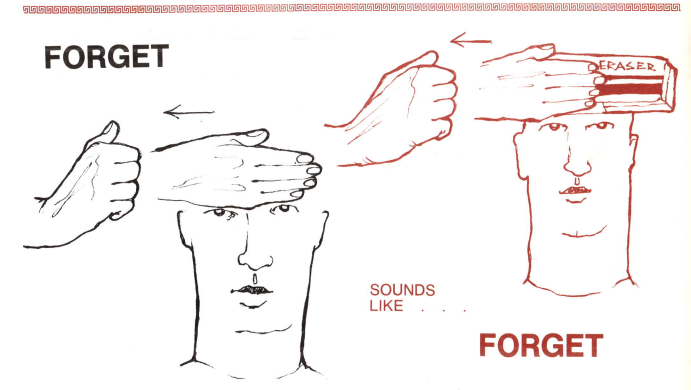

ERASER

SOUNDS LIKE . . . .

FORGET

IF YOU WERE TO <u>FORGET</u> YOU WOULD ERASE THE THOUGHT FROM YOUR BRAIN.

HOUSE

SOUNDS
LIKE . . .

HOUSE

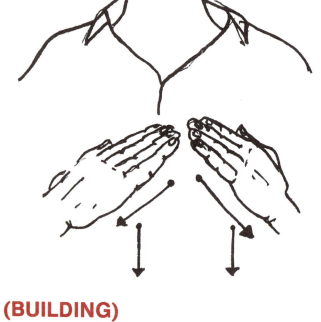

(BUILDING)

YOUR HANDS WILL SHAPE THE ROOF OF THE **HOUSE.**

TREE

SOUNDS
LIKE . . .

TREE

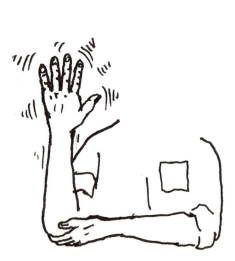

PICTURE YOUR RIGHT ARM AS A **TREE** AND YOUR WIGGLING FIN-
GERS AS BRANCHES.

TRY

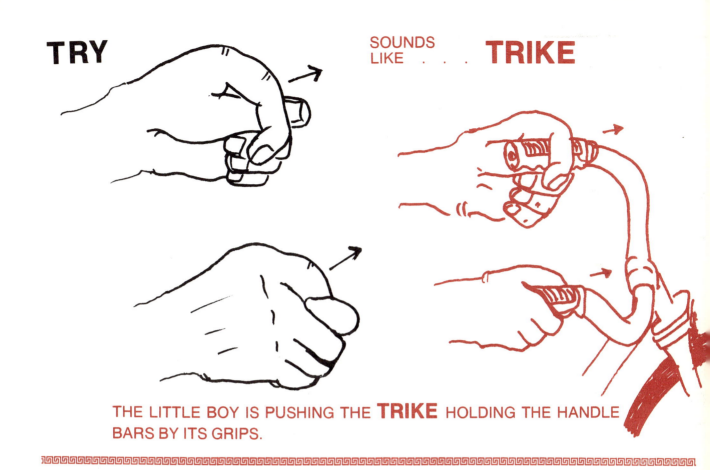

SOUNDS LIKE . . . **TRIKE**

THE LITTLE BOY IS PUSHING THE **TRIKE** HOLDING THE HANDLE BARS BY ITS GRIPS.

DO

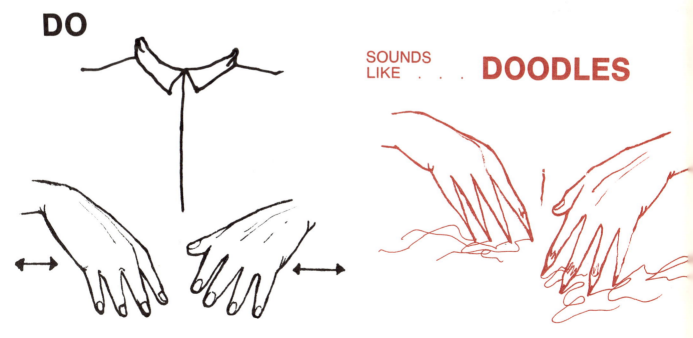

SOUNDS LIKE . . . **DOODLES**

THE FINGERS OF BOTH HANDS HAVE TURNED TO PENS AND THEY ARE **DOODLING** ON THE DESK.

You have just memorized these signs:

on	down
off	with
Large, big	together
Small, little	over
open	forget
close	house
in	tree
out	try
up	do

PRACTICE SENTENCES

(Spell the words that are underlined.)

1. Try to do it right for a change.
2. Mother can <u>hold</u> it over the table
3. The doctor and teacher can go together.
4. The girl is the kind to forget.
5. Take the small tree from my house.
6. Open the big book.
7. Close the house in the <u>summer</u>.
8. You can go up with the boy.
9. The teacher has to go down.
10. Why do you take it on and off?

LESSON 8

MUST

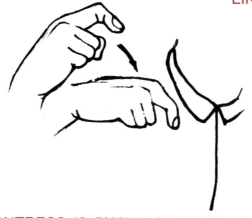

SOUNDS
LIKE . . . **MUSTARD**

THE WAITRESS IS PUSHING HER FINGER INTO A JAR OF **MUSTARD.**

(NEED, OUGHT, SHOULD)

MANY

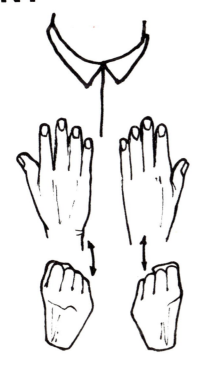

SOUNDS
LIKE . . . **MANEATER**

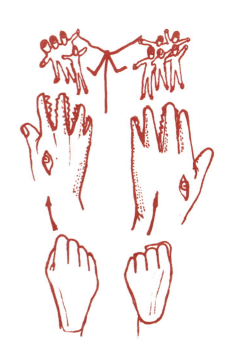

THE **MANEATER** is throwing **MANY** HANDFULS OF PEOPLE
INTO HIS MOUTH. HE DOES IT TWICE.

EASY

SOUNDS LIKE . . . **EASY CHAIR**

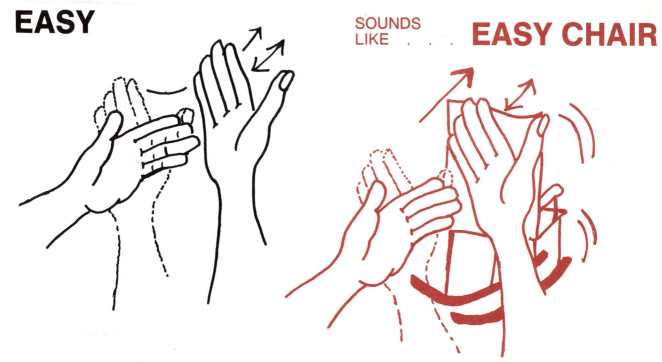

THE TWO HANDS START OUT OVERLAPPING; THEN THE BACK OF THE RIGHT PUSHES AN **EASY** CHAIR BACK AND FORTH.

HERE

SOUNDS LIKE . . . **EARS**

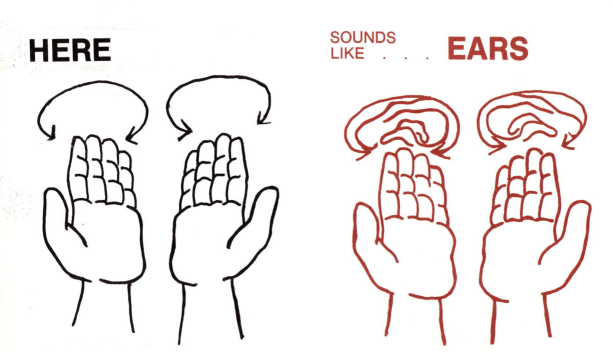

THE OUTSTRETCHED PALMS ARE RUBBING THE EDGES OF TWO **EARS.**

ABOUT

SOUNDS LIKE . . . **A BOWEL**

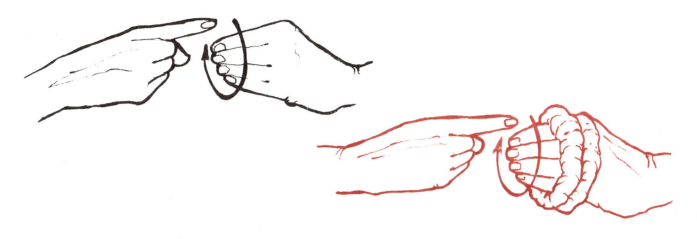

THE RIGHT INDEX FINGER IS WRAPPING A **BOWEL** AROUND THE LEFT HAND.

LATER

SOUNDS LIKE . . . **LAID HER**

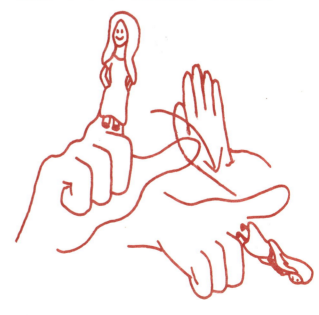

THE INDEX FINGER IS A GIRL WHO WAS STANDING AS THE UPPER PART OF LETTER 'L' — THEN THEY <u>LAID HER</u> DOWN.

FULL

SOUNDS LIKE . . . **FULL**

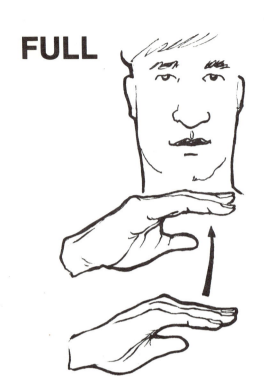

THE MAN IS **FULL**

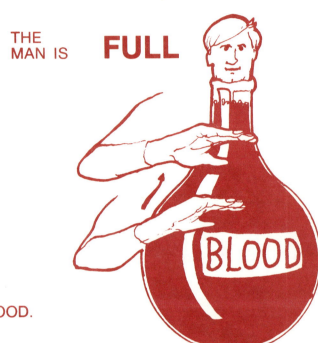

FULL UP TO THE NECK WITH BLOOD.

LONG

SOUNDS LIKE . . . **LONG**

A VERY LONG **LONG** ARM OF THE **LAW.**

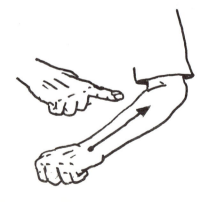

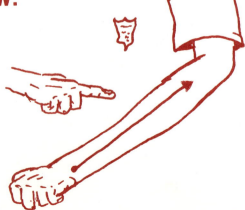

HARD

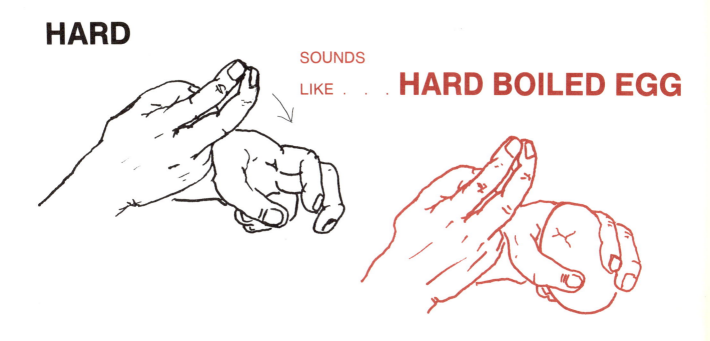

SOUNDS LIKE . . . **HARD BOILED EGG**

THE KNUCKLES OF THE RIGHT HAND ARE CRACKING A **HARD** BOILED EGG IN THE OTHER.

NEXT SOUNDS LIKE . . . **NECKS**

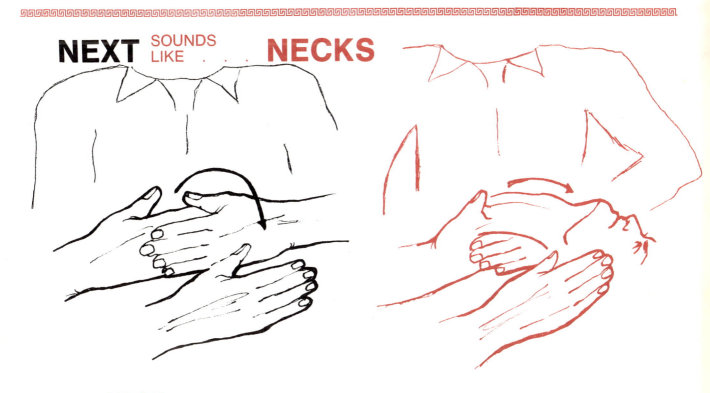

A **NECK** IS BEING STRETCHED FROM NEXT TO THE CHEST OUT AWAY FROM IT.

ASK

SOUNDS LIKE . . . **AX**

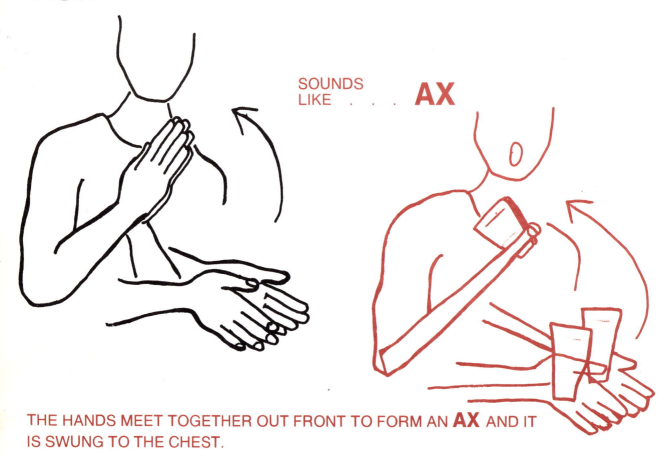

THE HANDS MEET TOGETHER OUT FRONT TO FORM AN **AX** AND IT IS SWUNG TO THE CHEST.

WANT

SOUNDS LIKE . . . **WANT ADS**

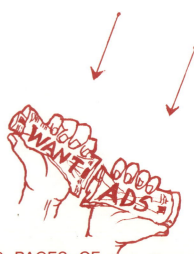

PICTURE A PERSON REACHING AND GRABBING 2 PAGES OF **WANT—ADS** AND PULLING THEM TO HIMSELF.

BUY

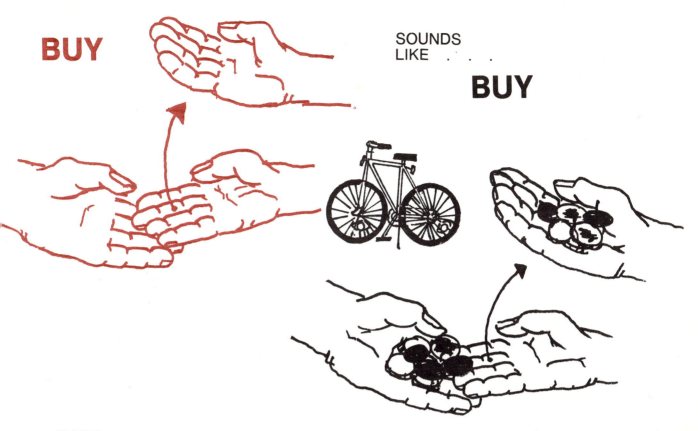

SOUNDS
LIKE . . .

BUY

TO **BUY** A BIKE YOU MUST SCOOP THE MONEY OUT OF ONE HAND
AND OFFER IT.

PLEASE

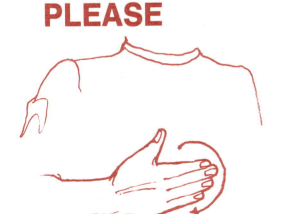

SOUNDS
LIKE . . . **PLEATS**

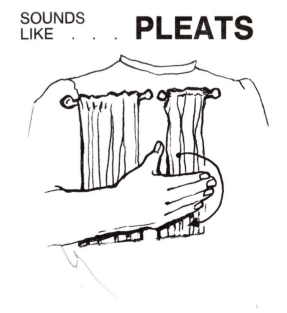

THE LADY IS FEELING THE **PLEATS** IN HER DRESS THAT IS MADE
OUT OF A CURTAIN THAT HAS MANY **PLEATS** ON IT. SHE IS
FEELING IT WITH BOTH HANDS.

PEOPLE

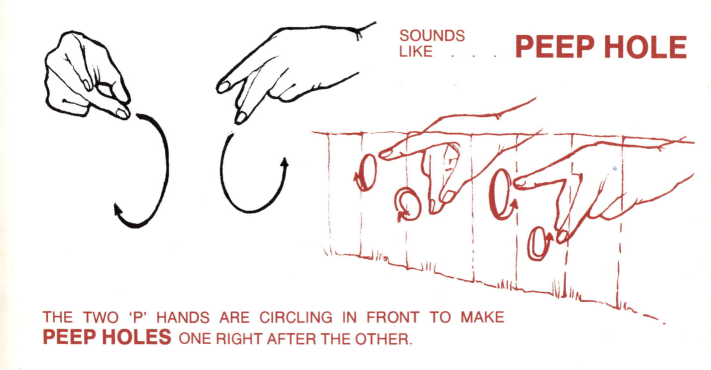

SOUNDS
LIKE . . . **PEEP HOLE**

THE TWO 'P' HANDS ARE CIRCLING IN FRONT TO MAKE
PEEP HOLES ONE RIGHT AFTER THE OTHER.

BRING

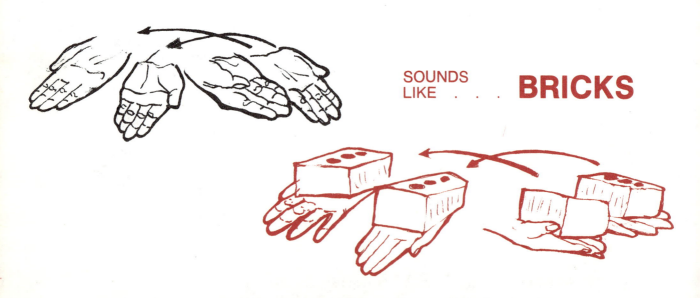

SOUNDS
LIKE . . . **BRICKS**

THE PERSON IS **BRING**ING **BRICKS** FROM ONE STACK TO ANOTHER.

USE

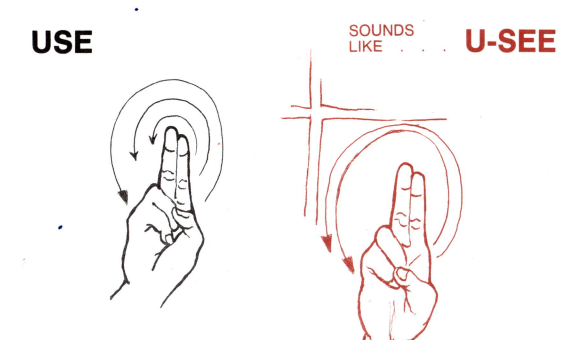

YOU CAN SEE THROUGH THE WINDOW BETTER WHEN YOU WIPE IT OFF WITH THE LETTER 'U' HAND, WIPING IN CIRCLES.

SAY, (SAID, SPOKE)

SOUNDS LIKE **SAY**

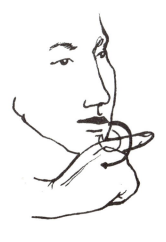 

SEE THE WORDS COMING OUT OF HER MOUTH.

You have just memorized these signs:

must	next
many	ask
easy	want
here	buy
about	please
later	people
full	bring
long	use
hard	say

PRACTICE SENTENCES

(Spell the words that are underlined.)

1. It is easy to sign and fingerspell.
2. You must bring it here.
3. People <u>will</u> ask about your idea.
4. Many people say it is hard.
5. You can use it later.
6. The girl can buy it next time.
7. Please bring it here.
8. The boy <u>will</u> say no to your offer.
9. The glass is full <u>of</u> cold water.
10. The girl can wait for a long time.

BREAK

SOUNDS LIKE . . . **BRACELET**

A PERSON IS GRABBING A **BRACELET** AND **BREAKING IT APART.**

BELOW

SOUNDS LIKE . . . **BEES LOWER**

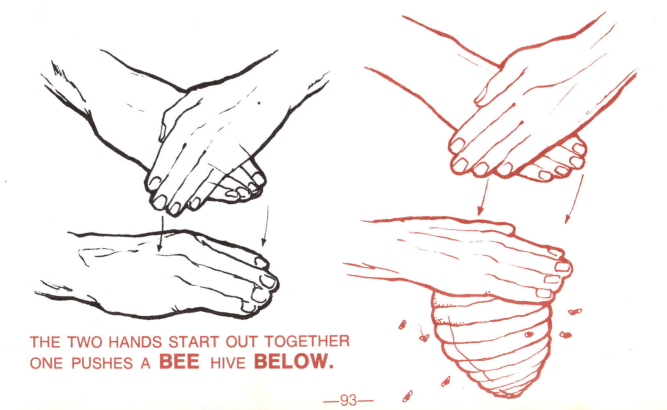

THE TWO HANDS START OUT TOGETHER ONE PUSHES A **BEE** HIVE **BELOW.**

ABOVE

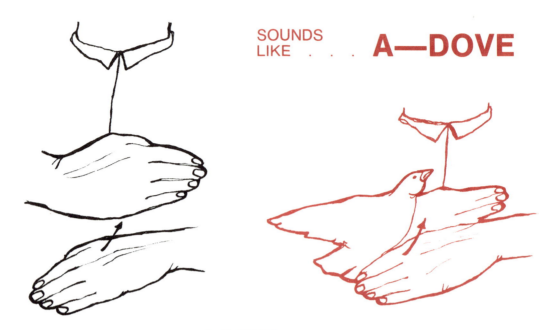

SOUNDS
LIKE . . . **A—DOVE**

THE ONE HAND IS **A DOVE** FLYING OFF OF THE OTHER.

OTHER

SOUNDS
LIKE . . . **OTTER**

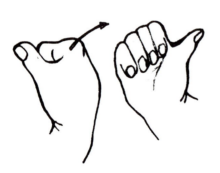 

SEE THE **OTTER** THAT IS STANDING ON THE ROAD HITCHHIKING.

SIT, **SEAT, CHAIR**

SOUNDS LIKE . . . **SIT**

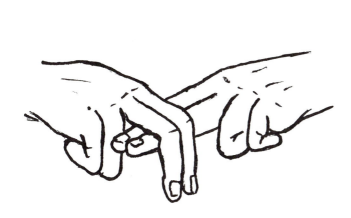

SEE THE MAN **SITTING** IN THE CHAIR — HIS LEGS HANGING OVER ARE YOUR FINGERS.

RIDE

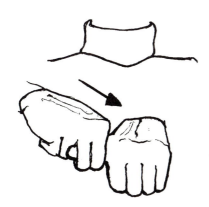

SOUNDS LIKE . . . **RIDE**

SEE THE MAN **RID**ING IN A **RID**ER BUS.

CAR

SOUNDS
LIKE . . . **CAR**

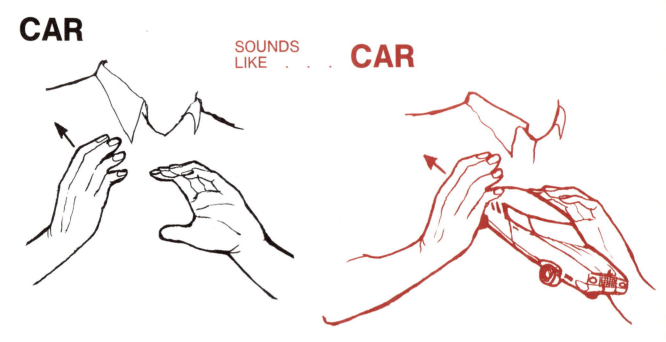

THE DRIVER IS POLISHING A SMALL **CAR** IN HIS HANDS.

TRAIN

SOUNDS
LIKE . . . **TRAIN**

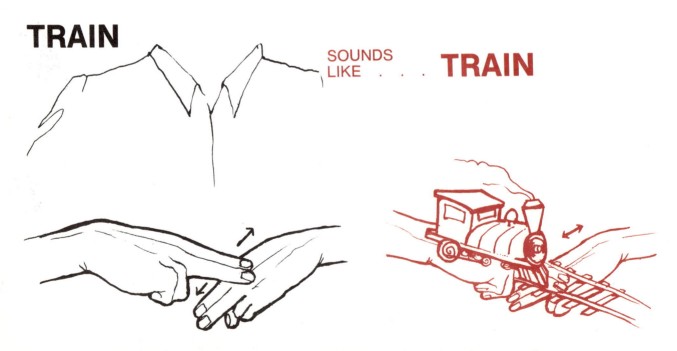

A **TRAIN** IS MOVING BACK AND FORTH ON THE TRACKS.(Your fingers are two tracks.)

BOAT

SOUNDS LIKE . . .

BOAT

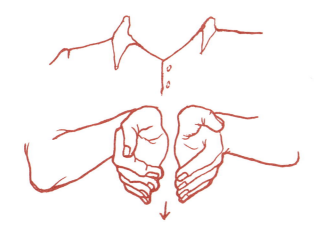

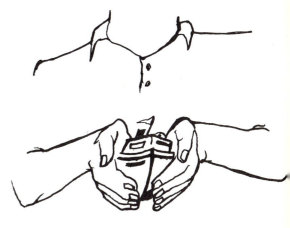

YOUR HANDS SHAPE THE HULL OF A BOAT IN FRONT OF YOU.

BICYCLE

SOUNDS LIKE . . .

BICYCLE

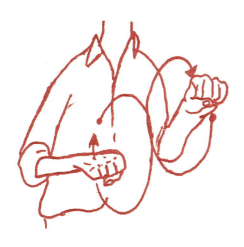

PICTURE A BICYCLE HANGING ABOVE YOU AND YOU ARE PEDDLING IT WITH YOUR HANDS.

AIRPLANE

SOUNDS LIKE . . .

AIRPLANE

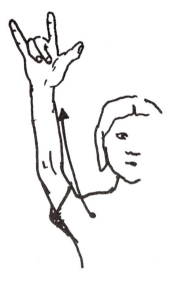

YOUR HAND IS LIKE AN **AIRPLANE**—IT HAS WINGS.

DRIVE

SOUNDS LIKE . . .

DRIVING

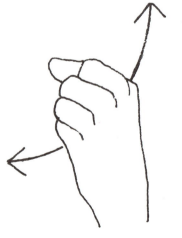

PICTURE A STEERING WHEEL IN YOUR FISTS AND TURN IT BACK AND FORTH. THIS WHEEL IS **DRIVING** THE CAR.

HURRY

HURDLE

LIKE TWO **HURDLERS** HURRYING AWAY FROM THE BODY JUMPING **HURDLES.**

ANY

SOUNDS LIKE . . .

A KNEE

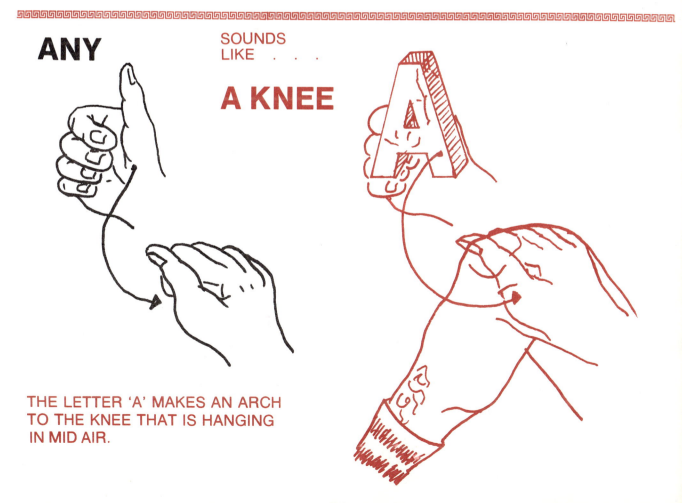

THE LETTER 'A' MAKES AN ARCH TO THE KNEE THAT IS HANGING IN MID AIR.

LIE

SOUNDS LIKE . . .

LIE

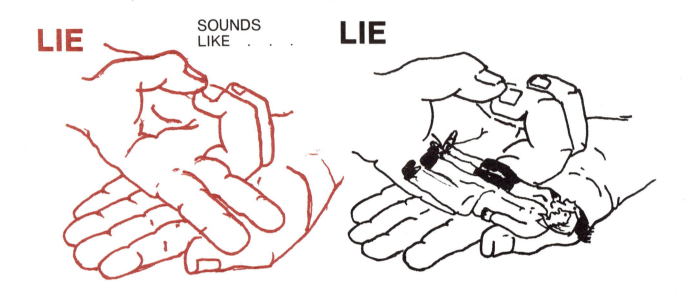

(LAY) THE FIRST TWO FINGERS HAVE TURNED INTO PEOPLE WHO ARE GOING TO **LIE** DOWN IN THE PALM OF THE OTHER HAND.

STAY

SOUNDS LIKE . . . **STEAKS**

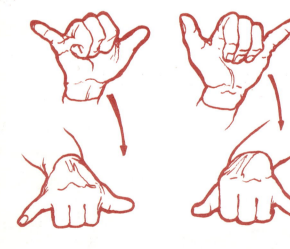

HOLDING TWO **STEAKS** UP WITH THE **'Y'** HANDS AND THEN FLOPPING THEM ON THE TABLE.

THAT

SOUNDS LIKE . . . **TAT, TAP, TAT**

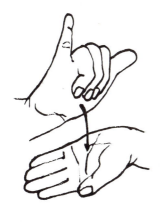 

SEE THE **TAP** DANCER'S SHOES ON THE ENDS OF THE FINGERS DANCING IN THE PALM GOING **TAT TAT.**

KEEP

SOUNDS LIKE . . . **KEYBOARDS**

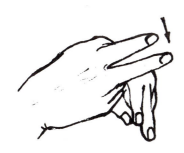 

CAN YOU PLAY TWO **KEYBOARDS** IN DIFFERENT DIRECTIONS.

You have just memorized these signs:

break	bicycle
below	airplane
above	drive
other	hurry
sit	any
ride	lie
car	stay
train	that
boat	keep

PRACTICE SENTENCES
(Spell the words that are underlined.)

1. That is the right train.
2. Thank the boy for the ride.
3. Hurry and drive the car here.
4. You can <u>not</u> sit in the other boat.
5. The girl <u>did not</u> break any cups.
6. The airplane can stay below the <u>clouds</u>.
7. Keep the bicycle above the chair.
8. You can keep your coat on any table.
9. Lie on the small book.
10. Who is your teacher?

VERY

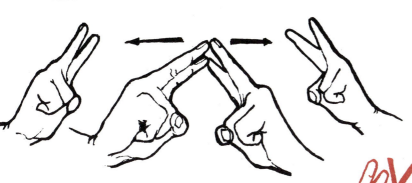

WITH THE 'V' HAND THE 'V's ARE **VERY** CLOSE
THEN **VERY** FAR AWAY

PUT

SOUNDS
LIKE . . . **PUTT**

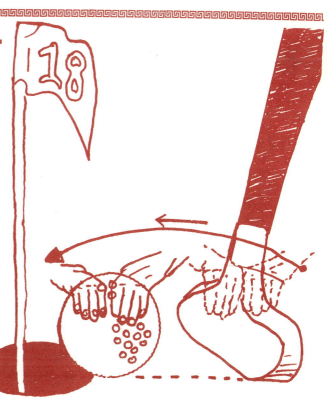

PICKING A BALL UP AND **PUTT**ING IT IN THE HOLE IS LIKE PUTT—
ING.

WILL

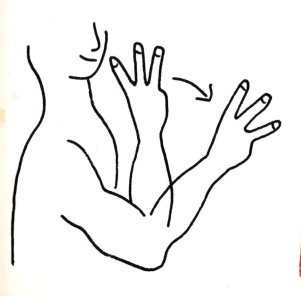

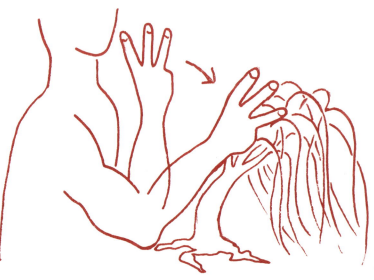

PICTURE A **WILLOW TREE** BEING PUSHED OVER WITH THE FLAT OF THE **w** HAND.

FEEL

SOUNDS LIKE . . . **FEET**

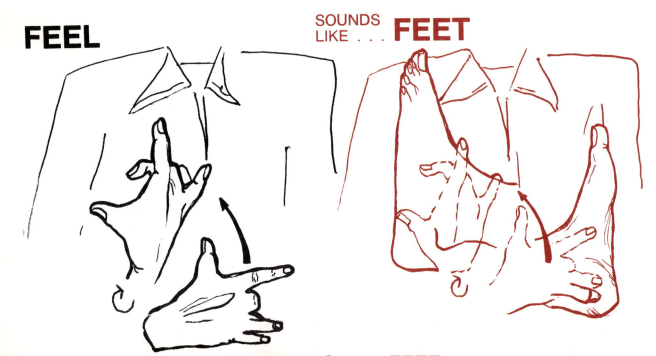

PICTURE A PERSON **FEELING** TWO **FEET** WITH THE MIDDLE FINGERS OF BOTH HANDS.

LIKE

SOUNDS LIKE . . . **LIME**

THE COOK IS GRABBING A **LIME** OUT IN FRONT OF THE BODY AND PULLING IT TO THE RIGHT.

AT

SOUNDS LIKE . . . **ATLANTIC OCEAN**

THE HAND HAS TURNED TO WAVES ON THE **ATLANTIC** AND IS WAVING IN FRONT OF THE CHEST UNTIL IT IS STOPPED BY THE OTHER HAND.

NOW

SOUNDS
LIKE . . . **KNOCKS**

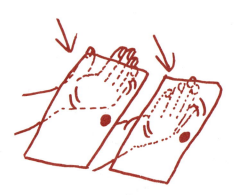

THE TWO HANDS WILL **KNOCK** ON TWO HORIZONTAL DOORS.

HAPPY

SOUNDS
LIKE . . . **HAPPY**

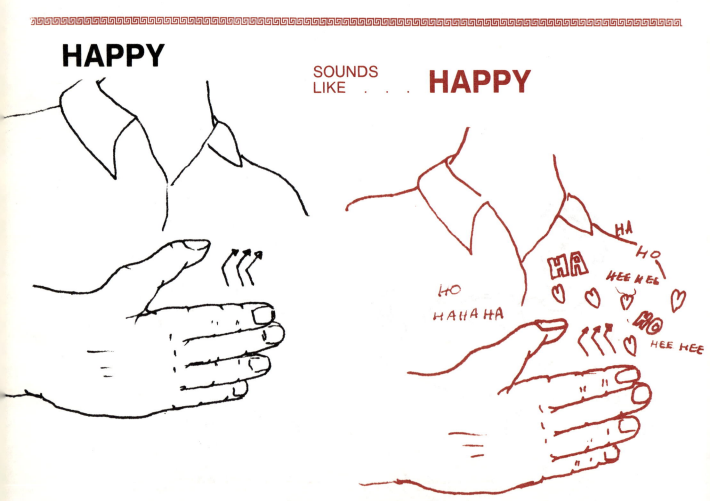

THE PERSON IS GETTING A **HAPPY** FEELING FROM RUBBING HIS CHEST.

SMILE

SOUNDS LIKE . . .

SMILE

LOOK AT THAT 'BIG' SMILE.

CRY

SOUNDS LIKE . . .

CRY

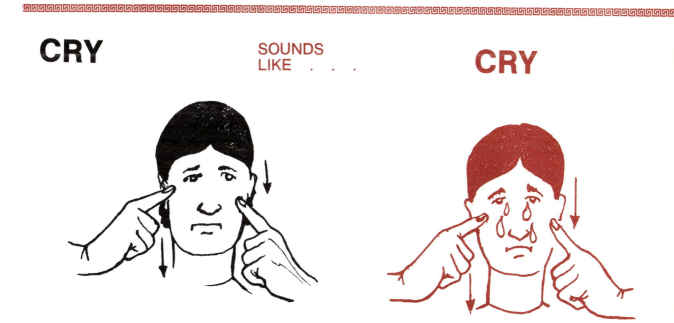

THE PERSON IS CRYING BY PULLING TEARS DOWN HER CHEEKS.

THING

SOUNDS
LIKE . . .

THINGS

THING ← THING

THINGS, THINGS, THINGS OUT IN THE HAND·

DROP

SOUNDS
LIKE . . .

DROPS

AS THE HANDS OPEN—**DROPS**
FALL OFF OF ALL THE FINGERS
AND THUMBS.

—108—

EACH

EAGLE

THE **EAGLE** IS FALLING OFF THE OTHER THUMB.

ALL

ALBUM

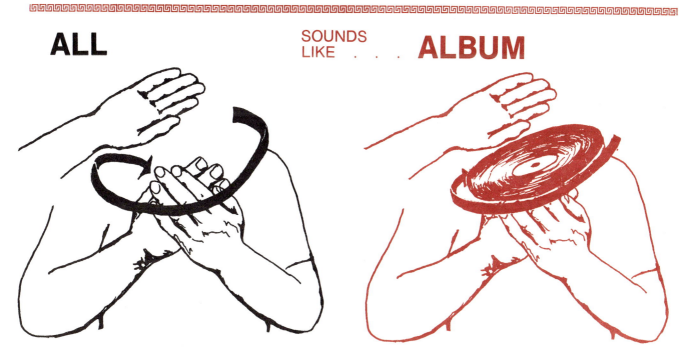

THE FINGERS ARE OVERLAPPED AND CIRCLING A RECORD **ALBUM.** IT HAS A **WHOLE** IN THE CENTER.

(WHOLE)

THINK

SOUNDS
LIKE . . .
THINK

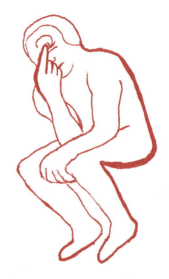

SEE THE MAN
SITTING AND TRYING
TO **THINK**
HE CIRCLES HIS INDEX
FINGER ON HIS HEAD
WHILE HE **THINKS.**

NOT

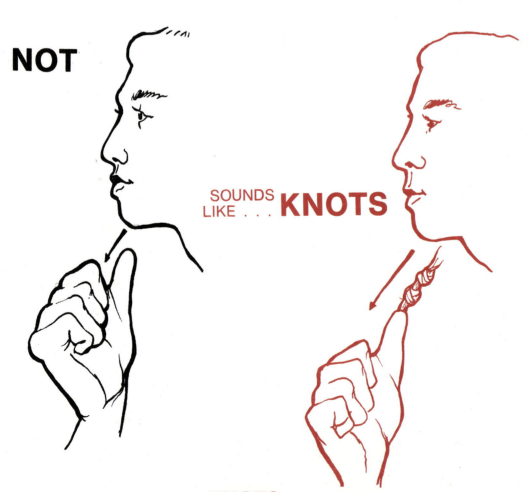

SOUNDS
LIKE . . . **KNOTS**

THE THUMB IS PULLING **KNOTS** OUT OF THE CHIN.

BEFORE

SOUNDS LIKE . . . **BEEF ORDER**

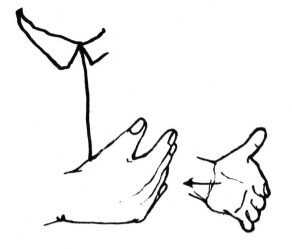 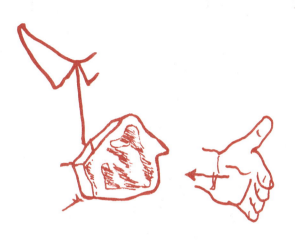

THE **BEEF ORDER** IS **BEFORE** THE OTHER HAND.

BETWEEN

SOUNDS LIKE . . . **BETWEEN**

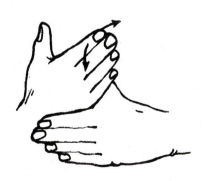 

TRYING TO WIGGLE YOUR HAND **BETWEEN** THE THUMB AND FINGERS OF THE LEFT HAND.

You have just memorized these signs:

will	put
feel	thing
smile	drop
cry	each
now	all
happy	before
like	between
at	think
very	not

PRACTICE SENTENCES

(Spell the words that are underlined.)

1. Put all the clothing in here.
2. How do you feel now?
3. The girl will cry when you meet.
4. The dentist will drop each thing.
5. Before you do it you must think.
6. I like to be happy.
7. Mother will not smile at you.
8. It is a long time between lunch and dinner.
9. That is a very good paper.
10. Each person must sign a new word.

Bibliography

Barnstein, H., Hamilton, L., Saulnier, K., Roy, Howard (Eds)***The Signed English Dictionary.*** Washington, D.C.: Gallaudet College Press, 1975

Fant, Louie J.,***Say it with Hands.*** Washington, D.C.: American Annals of the Deaf, Gallaudet College, 1964

Gustafson, G., Pfetzing, D., Zawolkow, E.***Signing Exact English.*** Maryland. The National Association of the Deaf, 1975

Huffman, Hoffman, Gransee, Fox, James, Schmitz, California State Department of Health, ***Sign Language for Everyone.*** California. Joyce Motion Picture Co., 1975

O'Rourke, T.,***A Basic Course in Manual Communication.*** Maryland. The National Association of the Deaf, 1975

Riekehof, Lottie L., ***The Joy of Signing.*** Missouri. Gospel Publishing House, 1978.

Watson, David O.,***Talk with your Hands.*** Wisconsin, G. Banta. 1973

INDEX

A...10
ABOUT.....................................85
ABOVE.....................................94
AIRPLANE..................................98
ALL......................................109
AM..19
AN..10
AND.......................................55
ANY.......................................99
ARE.......................................20
ASK.......................................88
AT.......................................105

BABY......................................25
BAD.......................................51
BE..21
BECAUSE...................................28
BEFORE...................................111
BELOW.....................................93
BETWEEN..................................111
BICYCLE...................................97
BIG.......................................74
BOAT......................................97
BOOK......................................38
BOWL......................................49
BOY.......................................24
BREAK.....................................93
BREAKFAST.................................43
BRING.....................................90
BROTHER...................................24
BUT.......................................53
BUY.......................................89
BY..10

CAN.......................................30
CAR.......................................96
CARRY.....................................89
CHAIR.....................................95
CHANGE....................................13
CHILDREN..................................61
CLOSE.....................................75
CLOTHING..................................65
COAT......................................65
COFFEE....................................58
COLD......................................39
COME......................................19
CUP.......................................48
CRY......................................107

DENTIST...................................36
DINNER....................................44
DO..81
DOCTOR....................................35
DOWN......................................77
DRINK.....................................45
DRIVE.....................................98
DROP.....................................108

EACH.....................................109
EASY......................................84
EAT.......................................45
EITHER....................................10

FATHER....................................34
FEEL.....................................104
FINGERSPELL...............................14
FIRE......................................68
FOR.......................................29
FORGET....................................79
FORK......................................46
FROM......................................61
FULL......................................86

GET.......................................57
GIRL......................................24
GIVE......................................53
GLASS.....................................48
GO..18
GOOD......................................50

HAPPY....................................106
HARD......................................87
HAVE......................................41
HE..10
HELP......................................70
HER.......................................10
HERE......................................84
HI..10
HIM.......................................10
HIS.......................................10
HOSPITAL..................................36
HOUSE.....................................80
HOW.......................................27
HURRY.....................................99

I...21
IDEA......................................23
IN..76
IS..20
IT..30

KEEP.....................................101
KEY.......................................33
KIND......................................55
KNIFE.....................................47

LARGE.....................................74
LATER.....................................85
LIE......................................100
LIKE.....................................105
LITTLE....................................74
LONG......................................86
LUNCH.....................................44

MAKE	70
MANY	83
ME	16
MEET	41
MILK	59
MORE	50
MOTHER	34
MUCH	56
MUST	83
MY	17
MYSELF	71

NAME	39
NEW	43
NEXT	87
NO	13
NOT	110
NOW	106
NURSE	35

OF	10
OFF	73
OFFER	88
ON	73
OPEN	75
OR	10
OTHER	94
OUT	76
OVER	79

PANTS	66
PAPER	38
PAY	63
PEOPLE	90
PERSON	16
PLATE	47
PLEASE	89
PUT	103

READ	37
RIDE	95
RIGHT	31

SAID	91
SAME	17
SANDWICH	58
SAY	91
SCHOOL	51
SEAT	95
SEE	40
SHE	10
SHOES	66
SHOWER	67
SIGN	14
SISTER	24
SIT	95
SMALL	74

SMILE	107
SO	10
SOAP	68
SOME	71
SPOKE	91
SPOON	46
STAND	40
STAY	100

TABLE	60
TAKE	54
TEACHER	33
TELEPHONE	69
THANK	63
THAT	101
THE	31
THEIR	10
THESE	10
THING	108
THINK	110
THIS	10
THOSE	10
TIME	69
TO	56
TOGETHER	78
TOILET	49
TRAIN	96
TREE	80
TRY	81

UNDER	57
UP	77
USE	91

VERY	103

WAIT	64
WALK	54
WANT	88
WASH	67
WATER	59
WE	29
WHAT	25
WHEN	26
WHERE	27
WHO	28
WHY	26
WILL	104
WITH	78
WORD	15
WORK	18
WRITE	37
WRONG	60

YES	23
YOU	15
YOUR	64

PUBLISHED BY:

    DILL ENTERPRISES
    P.O. BOX 29192
    LINCOLN, NE 68529

14
DAY
BOOK

This book may be kept
for 14 days only
It cannot be renewed

NT MAR 27 1985	F JAN 21 198		
MAR 22 1985	E APR 1 1987		
APR 22	E MAY 12 1987		
APR 22	E JUN 4 1987		
NT JUL 23 1985	E JUL 28 1987		
E FEB 5 1985	E SEP 15 1987		
E SEP 26 1985	F OCT 7 1987		
E OCT 30 1985	E OCT 29 1987		
E NOV 21			
E MAR 19 1986			
E APR 21 1986			
F MAY 8 1986			
F MAY 27 1986			
F JUL 28 1986			
E AUG 25 1986			
AUG 25			
E OCT 30 1986			
E DEC 16 1986			

GAYLORD   PRINTED IN U.S.A.